PRAISE FOR *HOPE RISING*

"*Hope Rising* not only proclaims a call to believe that extreme poverty can end in our lifetime, it also provides an inspiring path for each of us to make the fight personal and do our part. *Hope Rising* is worthy to be read. Worthy to be believed. And worthy to be acted on!"

SANTIAGO "JIMMY" MELLADO, PRESIDENT AND
CEO, COMPASSION INTERNATIONAL

"*Hope Rising* had a major impact on my thinking and is a must read for Christians who care about the poor. Dr. Todd moves beyond emotional appeals and guilt-based action to show solid reasons for generosity and the impact of wise, redemptive giving. The evidence presented in *Hope Rising* deserves a prominent place in our thinking and conversation on global poverty as we mobilize the Church toward getting to zero."

DAVID WILLS, PRESIDENT, NATIONAL CHRISTIAN FOUNDATION

"My heart started beating fast as Scott Todd laid out a bold vision for what our world could look like in 2035. I defy you to read this book without being awakened, stirred up, and all ready to sign up for the revolution to join our collective forces in God's name to end extreme poverty."

NANCY BEACH, LEADERSHIP COACH, THE SLINGSHOT GROUP
AUTHOR OF *GIFTED TO LEAD: THE ART OF
LEADING AS A WOMAN IN THE CHURCH*

"A refreshing, even daring new perspective—extreme poverty doesn't have to exist! Here's a book that converts the skeptical and energizes the church. There's no place for extreme poverty to hide from the power of God's people."

DR. WESS STAFFORD, PRESIDENT EMERITUS, COMPASSION INTERNATIONAL

"I couldn't put your book down. It was so refreshing. Not 'pie-in-the-sky,' but challenging to recognize the real needs in our world and hopeful that we can do this in our lifetime. The real prophet brings not just the bad news of judgment, but also the good news of restoration."

DR. MICHAEL D. SANDERS, PROFESSOR OF CHRISTIAN
FORMATION AND CAMPUS PASTOR, WARNER UNIVERSITY

"*Hope Rising* both strikes a chord and hits a nerve. It is insightful and provocative. It will help many people break free from the 'low expectations' trap."

JOHN ORTBERG, SENIOR PASTOR OF MENLO PARK PRESBYTERIAN CHURCH AND AUTHOR OF *THE ME I WANT TO BE*

"*Hope Rising* turns conventional thinking about poverty on its head and invites us to follow Christ in ways that profoundly change the world."

STEPHEN BAUMAN, PRESIDENT/CEO, WORLD RELIEF

"*Hope Rising* will change many hearts and empower the church to rise up to put an end to extreme poverty! I am now a believer that God can end extreme poverty through His people!"

GEORGE BOCOX, PASTOR OF NEW HOPE EVANGELICAL CHURCH, MCPHERSON, KANSAS

"*Hope Rising* is practical, inspirational, motivating, and challenging. Without overwhelming the reader, Todd presents the problem and paths toward a solution. After reading this book, you will take the issue of poverty personally."

DALE HANSON BOURKE, AUTHOR, *THE SKEPTIC'S GUIDE TO GLOBAL POVERTY*

"Do you sometimes wonder if there's really any hope of ending poverty, or if God wants you to do anything about it? If so, read *Hope Rising*, be inspired, join the 58: initiative, let God draw you into 'His desire to heal the world' and become part of what Scott Todd calls this 'uncrushable movement' to end global poverty. With arguments and stories that are in turn both hard-hitting and lovely, Dr. Todd explains why God cares for the poor, why we should care too, and how we can join a movement within Christ's church that is truly having a global impact."

DR. ROLAND HOKSBERGEN, ECONOMIST AND DIRECTOR, INTERNATIONAL DEVELOPMENT STUDIES PROGRAM AT CALVIN COLLEGE

"Dr. Scott Todd delivered one of the best presentations I've seen at Q . . . The data are convincing, the call is compelling . . . Scott is architecting one of the great efforts of the global church."

GABE LYONS, AUTHOR OF *THE NEXT CHRISTIANS* AND FOUNDER OF Q

"Scott Todd's *Hope Rising* presents a bold and compelling view of what it means to live as a Christian in an age of poverty and globalization. What can Christians in rich countries do about poverty? Todd not only shows what the churches can do to fight poverty, but provides a biblical basis for the roles of business and government. *Hope Rising* is a passionate, personalized narrative that will challenge the individual Christian, but is also suitable for study in small groups of believers who want to work together to make a positive difference for the poor in Jesus' name."

BRUCE WYDICK, PHD, PROFESSOR OF ECONOMICS,
UNIVERSITY OF SAN FRANCISCO, AND VISITING PROFESSOR,
UNIVERSITY OF CALIFORNIA AT BERKELEY

"I loved, loved, loved it!"

ROBIN HERSMA, MOTHER OF FOUR AND FOSTER PARENT

"*Hope Rising* is a compelling call to have followers of Jesus Christ fast-forward the end of extreme poverty. Scott Todd is a modern-day William Wilberforce who brings passion, Scripture, and strategy to ignite the church for world-changing action."

PETER GREER, PRESIDENT/CEO, HOPE INTERNATIONAL

"*Hope Rising* is a call to the church to throw off the low expectations that limit our vision and hope for what the Maker of the universe can and will do through us. Let's heed the invitation to roll up our sleeves and join God in the miraculous works He has prepared for us to do."

JIM MARTIN, VICE PRESIDENT OF SPIRITUAL
FORMATION, INTERNATIONAL JUSTICE MISSION

"Are you overwhelmed by global poverty? This book proves that the end of extreme poverty is closer than we think—and each of us can join in today's movement. Extreme poverty has been cut in half in the last thirty years, and the global church is the most promising force to bring it to an end. The church led the abolition of slavery, and in our generation we will lead the abolition of extreme poverty. *Hope Rising* offers a hopeful invitation to each of us to be the movement that puts global poverty into the history books."

RICH HALVORSON, FOUNDER, GLOBAL FAST

"As a community of faith we are guilty of low expectations concerning the Lord's ability to use His body to restore and redeem His creation. After reading *Hope Rising* I was convicted and encouraged by the simplicity of the solution and the vision of the future that should be ours as followers of Christ. The strategy outlined by Dr. Todd is a necessary reminder of why the Body exists and provokes individuals to respond to the call of Christ."

ERIC E. PRATT, PH.D., VICE PRESIDENT FOR CHRISTIAN DEVELOPMENT, MISSISSIPPI COLLEGE

"Get ready to be uncomfortable. Scott Todd applies the message and spirit of the Jewish prophets to the call of the church today. *Hope Rising* insists on linking love for God with the work of ending preventable human suffering caused by extreme poverty. Inspired by an optimism grounded in Scripture, *Hope Rising* offers practical strategies to make the end of the worst forms of poverty an achievable reality in our day."

DON GOLDEN, SENIOR VICE PRESIDENT OF MARKETING & CHURCH ENGAGEMENT, WORLD RELIEF

"For too many, it's easy to become hopeless about the state of the world's poor. Dr. Scott Todd challenges this stance, taking us on a fascinating tour of extreme poverty through recent history, showing us glimmers of hope, and calling this generation of Christ-followers to work together to end extreme poverty in our lifetime. We are already winning, and with concerted effort, extreme poverty can indeed be history."

CHAD HAYWARD, EXECUTIVE DIRECTOR, ACCORD NETWORK

"This is a book to launch a movement. In *Hope Rising*, Scott Todd has a bold and prophetic voice, calling us to escape the tyranny of our own low expectations. Children don't have to die from hunger or preventable diseases. God has given us all the tools we need to defeat extreme poverty. Having worked in the fight against poverty for nearly twenty years, I confess that I approached *Hope Rising*'s basic premise—that the poor need not always be with us—with skepticism. Yet I was quickly convicted regarding my own complacency and lack of hope. In bite-sized and easily digestible chapters, Todd makes a very compelling case that we can do much more to help the poor and in fact have already had much more success than we realize. The vision he casts, a vision of a church that will practice the true fast of Isaiah 58, is thrilling and a vision we can all get behind. It is a vision that just may transform the North American church even as it transforms the world."

SCOTT SABIN, EXECUTIVE DIRECTOR, PLANT WITH PURPOSE

HOPE
RISING

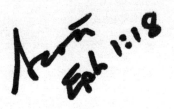

Eph 1:18

H⊕PE RISING

HOW **CHRISTIANS** CAN END **EXTREME** **POVERTY** IN THIS GENERATION

SCOTT TODD

NELSON BOOKS

An Imprint of Thomas Nelson

Published in Nashville, Tennessee, by Nelson Books, an imprint of Thomas Nelson. Nelson Books and Thomas Nelson are registered trademarks of HarperCollins Christian Publishing, Inc.

Thomas Nelson, Inc., titles may be purchased in bulk for educational, business, fund-raising, or sales promotional use. For information, please e-mail SpecialMarkets@ ThomasNelson.com.

The Library of Congress Cataloging-in-Publication Data is on file with the Library of Congress

ISBN-13: 978-0-5291-0112-9

Printed in the United States of America

14 15 16 17 18 RRD 6 5 4 3 2 1

In memory of Jacqueline
As a humble effort to keep my promise

CONTENTS

PART 4:
THE PRIMARY COLORS OF SOCIAL CHANGE

PART 5:
CATALYSTS AND STRATEGY

PART ONE

THE DEATH AND RESURRECTION OF EXPECTATIONS

CHAPTER 1

A NEW DAY FOR
STARFISH

n the late twentieth century there was a story written by Loren
Eiseley called "The Star Thrower" that became popular among
Christians. It goes like this:

> A man was walking along the beach when he saw a boy picking
> something up and throwing it into the ocean.
>
> Approaching the boy, he asked, "What are you doing?"
>
> "Throwing starfish back into the ocean," he said. "The
> surf is up, and the tide is going out. If I don't throw them back,
> they'll die."
>
> "Son," the man said, "don't you realize there are miles
> and miles of beach and hundreds of starfish? You can't make
> a difference!"
>
> After listening politely, the boy bent down, picked up
> another starfish, and threw it back into the surf. Then, smiling
> at the man, he said, "I made a difference for that one."

I've heard this story in several sermons—you probably have too. It's a sweet story with the message that you *can* make a difference, one at a time. But it is strong on individualism—individual action resulting in individual rescue.

Had the story been written for the twenty-first-century Christian, it would be quite different. Maybe it would go something like this:

A man was walking along the beach when he saw a girl taking a picture of a starfish with her iPhone.

Approaching the girl, he asked, "What are you doing?"

"Uploading pictures of these stranded starfish to my Facebook page and asking friends to tweet the call to action," she said. "The surf is up, and the tide is going out. If I can get enough friends out here, we can get all these starfish back into the water before sunset."

"Little girl," the man asked, "what does tweet mean?"

The girl rolled her eyes. She bent down, picked up a starfish, and threw it back into the surf. Then she gave the man a wry, twinkly-eyed smile and said, "If you want to help us out, this is how you do it."

Within hours, thousands of children stormed the beach, and every starfish was rescued.

The biggest difference between the man and the girl was what each of them expected. The man did not expect that all the starfish could be rescued—he expected them to die. He thought the problem was too big, that it was just reality for starfish. But the girl was not a hostage to such low expectations. And that made all the difference. Expecting that every starfish could be saved unleashed her exuberant action, while the man slumped critically upon the beach prophesying about life's impossibilities.

The girl didn't just expect the starfish to live—that would be wishful thinking. Instead she saw that she could do something. She made a plan and took action, and that is what hope is all about. Hope is the action-driving fuel that turns vision into reality.

But the story might continue:

As the last starfish was tossed into the ocean, the children celebrated their accomplishment on the beach. It had been a good day—for them and for the starfish.

But not all of them were playing. One boy faced the water, deep in thought.

The little girl approached him and asked, "What's up?"

Still gazing into the distance of ocean and imagination, he said, "How'd it happen in the first place?"

Turning to face the girl, eyes locking with hers in resolve, he continued, "And how do we make sure it never happens again?"

This is a book about getting a bunch of friends together to rescue all the starfish—every last one—*and* being faithful to each one. It's about building a world in which, once the starfish have been rescued, they will no longer be at risk. This is a book about hope. A gritty hope, rooted in reality, holding high expectations of the future and putting muscles to a plan of action to get there.

CHAPTER 2

WHY I WRITE

*Hope begins in the dark, the stubborn hope that if you
just show up and try to do the right thing, the dawn will
come. You wait and watch and work: You don't give up.*
—ANNE LAMOTT

I n 2005, I was the director of Compassion International's AIDS
Initiative, working to provide anti-retroviral medicine, the
medicine that stops HIV and treats AIDS, to the children in our
care. We had already seen great success in most of our African
countries—many kids were alive and playing again because of
those medicines. But somehow Tanzania was different. It was
resistant to our efforts.

I was on my knees in the Tanzanian dirt next to a twelve-year-
old girl named Jacqueline. Jacqueline had watched her mother and
father die slow, brutal deaths. She saw them lose weight. She saw the
sores break out. She listened to them coughing through the night
in their one-room mud hut, night after night for months on end.

Her father died first.

As her mother became too weak to walk, Jacqueline had to care for her. She fetched the firewood, searched for rice or cassava to cook, and fed the one who had once fed her. Her mother soon became too weak to get up. Jacqueline had to clean up her mother's diarrhea and was alone with her on the night the coughing stopped. After her mother died, Jacqueline was taken to live with her grandmother.

About a year later, Jacqueline, too, began to get sick. When she went to the clinic, the nurse told her she had "the sickness." HIV had been hiding in her body since birth. She heard again the chanting chorus that was part of the government's HIV education and prevention campaign: "AIDS is death! AIDS kills!" Except, for her, this was more than an HIV prevention song—it was her dirge.

She knew she would die like her parents.

The day I visited Jacqueline, she was lying on a mat outside her grandmother's mud hut. Her HIV infection had spread with unexpected speed, dismantling her immune system and leaving her defenseless to a host of other infections.

I knelt in the crusted dirt at Jacqueline's side and prayed for her. I prayed with optimism because the day before a local Christian hospital agreed to provide those lifesaving medicines for fifty-three children. Jacqueline was on that list. I prayed with hope that God would use the medicines to heal her, as I had seen Him do with so many other children. I prayed that we would have the privilege of watching Jacqueline become healthy and able to play. That we would hear her laugh again and watch her grow into a beautiful young lady.

The next day, I began the long journey home to the US, comforted by the knowledge that Jacqueline was on her way to the clinic to begin the treatment that would save her life.

But when I arrived home, a message was waiting for me. "Jacqueline is dead."

Those words hit me in the gut. They created an ache that I still feel. Everything she needed to get well had been in place for her. The story wasn't supposed to end like that. We did get her to the clinic, and we did begin therapy, but we were too late. Jacqueline's body had grown too weak, and she needed some basic strength in order for those medicines to revive her. We missed the opportunity to save her life, maybe by only a day.

I've been with many children who died—kids who were abused, abandoned, literally left to die. But it's Jacqueline's sweet voice that I still hear. It is her face that persists in my memory. It hurts. I wish I could go back and be there in time.

Since that moment on my knees in the dirt of Tanzania, I have had many sleepless nights, and I often think about Jacqueline. I know that although she died, she is now fully alive—she is immortal and with God. During one of those sleepless nights shortly after her death, I was remembering her and could see her face. I even felt that perhaps it wasn't her memory but her presence that was with me. I promised her that her death would not be in vain. I swore to do everything I could, with whatever influence God grants, to never be too late again.

That's why you're holding this book. So we'll be there in time, not just for children with HIV, but for all of them—every last one—whatever the infection or threat.

Each child is a gift, reflecting the image of her Creator, and God's love for each child must beat within us as well. He is unlikely to welcome us warmly if it doesn't (Matt. 25:31–46).

I'm not the only one who bears the burden of Jacqueline's death. The loss is not theirs or mine. It is *our* loss. We all bear this burden.

The weight of a child's preventable death is added to our shoulders nearly twenty thousand times every day. The burden of lost opportunity increases with each name added to the list. But we can choose to lift this weight. It's up to us to make this world a place where kids do not die from preventable causes.

Before we chart a course of action, we must confront a fundamental problem: many good people doubt that the weight can be lifted. Perhaps you doubt it too. Possible in theory, perhaps, but we don't expect success anytime soon. I understand that doubt. I've felt it too.

But it *is* possible. We even have a plan that *will* work. But before we can act on that plan, we must break free from the tyranny of low expectations. I want to lift your expectations of what is possible, the future, yourself, the church, even your expectations of God.

That won't come easily. Old expectations are like zombies that refuse to die, but they must die before new expectations can replace them.

Once new expectations fuel our efforts, we can put our plan into action. If we fail to move fast, however, exorcising our low expectations will be pointless—even dangerous. It'll be like the cast-out demon returning with seven demons more wicked than itself to find the man's soul still vacant (Luke 11:24–26). We must act quickly and credibly in this effort, or I fear a tsunami of cynicism will engulf us, and the zombies of low expectations will retrench.

The ideas in this book will move you to expect that Christians, by God's grace and power, will bring an end to extreme global poverty in the next twenty-one years. I believe we will build a world where massive numbers of children no longer die from mosquito bites, invisible killers in their water, or any other preventable threats. On the journey ahead, we will no longer slouch under mediocre expectations of God or of ourselves. Instead we will discover sources of unexpected hope and draw strength to do what God has equipped us to do.

CHAPTER 3

COLD SHOWERS OF UNMET EXPECTATIONS

Expect great things of God. Attempt great things for God.

—WILLIAM CAREY

The hotel bed sagged like a hammock under my jet-lagged body. My Timex beeped out the mantra, "Get up! The only time zone that matters is mine." I rolled off the bed in reluctant obedience and staggered to the bathroom. The sulfuric smell of the nation's sewer escaped the toilet, an unsubtle reminder of my distance from home.

I reached into the shower to crank on the water fully to the red side. Liquid burps and blasts spluttered from the showerhead. I waited for it to turn hot. It didn't. It wasn't cold-cold, just room temperature cold. "Just the way it is, I guess," I grumbled to myself and stepped in.

About seventy-eight seconds later, I grabbed a towel, which unfolded to reveal a large, yellowish-brown stain. Apart from air-drying, this degenerate towel was my one and only option, and I was already late. I dried off with a wary eye on the stain, dressed, and embarked on my day in Jayapura City on the easternmost island of Indonesia.

I knew I was in a poor city, but I still expected hot water and a clean towel. Not that I was aware of that expectation. Most of our expectations lurk below the surface of our conscious thoughts. They're there. No matter what time zone we're in or where we sleep, they're our traveling companions. When they're unmet, we get frustrated. We want an explanation.

I can hardly imagine what would happen in my house if my four boys came downstairs on a Christmas morning to discover that the tree had been abducted during the night, and there wasn't a present in sight. I would face a pajama-wearing, watery-eyed inquisition. My four-year-old would probably cry. Unmet expectations.

What if your employer said your next paycheck wouldn't be issued? What if your car didn't start? What if you were eager to watch your favorite football team, and the network showed the Florida shuffleboard championship instead? What if your son decided not to go to college? What if you were on the toilet, and you looked over to see only two squares of paper left on the roll? What if you had found your refrigerator inexplicably empty this morning? Did you expect to eat today?

Expectations are everywhere, and they exist whether you want them to or not. They escort every thought, and they set life's agenda. They are on the pillow next to us each morning. The sun will come up. I will eat. My car will start. My employer will pay me. My shower will spray hot water. My toilet paper roll will have more than two squares.

If these things don't happen, then our normally docile mental escorts become arsonists, lighting fires of frustration and discontent, starting riots and noisily demanding answers. Or, in mild situations such as insufficient toilet paper, they may at least mutter complaints.

Marriage counselors tell us that most of our conflicts arise from unmet expectations: She expected me to take out the trash. She expected me to remember our anniversary. She did not expect me to buy a boat without talking to her (I would never). Most challenges in work relationships are also rooted in unmet expectations. Your boss expected you to be at your desk on time. Maybe he wanted your project done by this morning but didn't make that clear when he assigned it to you. Maybe you expected him to communicate more clearly and own up to his mistakes.

An expectation is not the same as a wished-for future. Instead an expectation is an anticipated future that shapes today's decisions. If we expect the stock market to go up, then we buy (if we're rich enough to do so), but if we only *wish* for it to up, then we do nothing. Wishful thinking is a fantasy. Optimism is a mere attitude. Expectations, on the other hand, are probable, seemingly inevitable scenarios for our futures. Expectations provide a scaffold for our decision making, and we gamble on them every day.

I've mentioned a lot of mundane expectations, but what about the big ones, such as war and hunger? Did you expect extreme poverty to be gone by now?

Maybe that's why it isn't.

Maybe that's why we're not frustrated about extreme poverty. We're sad about it but not frustrated, let alone angry. We may sigh, but we don't demand answers. It's just the way it is . . . right?

I've heard good people say things like, "I mean, we should help the poor and care for the ones we can, but setting unrealistic expectations that we can end poverty will just come back to bite us."

We don't expect ourselves to end extreme poverty. We don't expect our governments to end it. We don't expect God to end it. Instead, we expect it to exist as it always has. It may even get worse.

I got back to my hotel in Jayapura City after fourteen hours of traveling to remote villages, sitting on dirt floors, and holding hands with barefoot children in tattered shirts. The heat, sweat, dust, and grime of the day clung to me. I again faced the burping shower, but this time with much more "realistic" (a.k.a. low) expectations. I cranked the handle fully to the red side again and waited. It produced the same unhappy result.

I had spent the day with kids whose parents had died. Who lived in places I couldn't pronounce. Places that did not have clean water to drink, let alone the luxury of a shower. They didn't have electricity or beds. I felt guilty as I stared at that burping showerhead—guilty that I could return to a hotel, guiltier still about my frustration over not having hot water. I'm not saying I should have felt guilty, but I did.

I don't know why, but I decided to crank the lever all the way over to blue. Maybe I thought I would take a cold shower as an act of solidarity or penance. Suddenly the water became piping hot.

I held my hand in the hot mist. *What an idiot*, I thought. I began my day frustrated that no matter how hard I cranked the handle, I couldn't get the hot water I expected from the red side. I never bothered to try blue. I briefly wondered if blue really meant hot in Indonesia. Then I decided that the guy who installed the lever put it in backward. Maybe that worker didn't have the daily opportunity to decide which way to crank his shower handle. Maybe he assumed that anyone could figure it out.

Looking back, I realize something important: I was not the victim of unmet expectations that morning. At first, I thought I expected hot water and got lukecold water. But I hadn't, really.

I had taken cues from my environment. I had listened to the testimonies of the sulfuric gasses from the toilet and of the burping showerhead. They told me that this place might not have hot water. So I was in fact the victim of low expectations—I got the cold water I expected. If I had expected hot water, I would have been relentless in my effort to get it. I would have certainly explored the blue side rather than believing a cold shower was just another bit of reality.

High expectations innovate. High expectations persevere. High expectations don't quit until they're satisfied.

CHAPTER 4

JACKI

Hope is faith holding out its hand in the dark.

—GEORGE ILES

After Jacqueline died I wrote her a letter, which I kept for four years until I was finally able to return to Tanzania. I planned to give a gift to Jacqueline's grandmother and tell her that Jacqueline's memory had been honored. Within one year of her death, Compassion was providing anti-retroviral medicine to every child in our program who needed them. I wanted to tell her that many others in Jacqueline's situation were being protected from the suffering she experienced. I planned to visit Jacqueline's grave and read the letter to her.

Here's what I wrote:

Dear Jacqueline,

I don't know how this works. I believe that you are in the arms of our loving Father now and maybe you are aware of all that is happening here. I wasn't able to be at your funeral.

When people die, we sometimes need to say some things to help us resolve our grief, and I guess that is what this letter is about for me.

I am reading it to a group of people who believed in your potential. Though they didn't know your name, your friends, or what made you laugh, they believe that God created you with great potential. They know that you were robbed. And we were robbed of the chance to see you grow into the beautiful woman that God intended.

It isn't fair. It isn't right. I hate that you suffered. I hate the pain you felt and every tear you shed alone in that mud hut. I hate the evils of the world that stole your life. I hate the complacency of Christians who could have done something about it. I hate that we weren't there earlier for you. That I wasn't there earlier. I was too late.

And I'm sorry. I let you down. I know you probably don't feel that way right now, being where you are with Him, but I still feel that way.

By God's grace I will not let you down again. I will not forget you, and I will do everything in my power, with whatever influence God gives me, to be there for the other kids. I believe I am standing in an army of Christ-followers who will join me in that promise.

With love, I look forward to holding your hand again.

Scott

I guess I thought reading this letter at Jacqueline's graveside would bring me closure. But my plans did not turn out.

Somehow there was a miscommunication with our Tanzanian staff, and the schedule made it difficult for me to see Jacqueline's grandmother. On the third day of the trip, we visited a church near Jacqueline's home, where I listened to a dozen children sing a powerful song about the importance of caring for those with HIV. The chorus was, "Do not oppress the orphan." A new and beautiful chorus compared to the chanting, "AIDS is death! AIDS kills!" I heard years earlier.

Afterward, we went to visit some of the children in their homes. The houses were small, so not everyone in our group could go in. I decided to stay outside. There was a girl nearby playing with a pink balloon, and I watched her bump it into the air and try to keep it from hitting the ground. An unexpected breeze stirred and pushed the balloon my way, and I hit it back up and toward the girl. We played the game together, bumping this pink balloon back and forth and smiling. It was a happy moment—until I accidentally hit the balloon up onto a chicken coop with a rusty metal roof.

Please don't pop! I begged silently. Wouldn't that be perfect— the white guy shows up and pops the girl's balloon. Thankfully it didn't. After its vulnerable dance on the rusty, corrugated tin, it fell to the ground. I picked it up and handed it to her. As she took the balloon from me, she looked into my eyes, and in a sweet but strong voice, she said, "Thank you."

In that moment, I felt something that's hard to explain, but I've felt it in other moments too—a kind of presence. Like a shimmer or gasp. I had sudden goose bumps.

I asked a nearby woman about the girl. Like Jacqueline, this girl was twelve years old. Like Jacqueline, her parents had both died from HIV. After their deaths, she, too, had been taken to live with her grandmother. The girl with the pink balloon was also HIV positive, born with the virus that everyone assumed would take her life. In fact, she was one of those fifty-three children on that list from four years earlier—on that same list with Jacqueline as one of the children who needed the anti-retroviral (ARV) medicine. I could hardly believe it! Compassion International has more than 30,000 kids in our programs just in Tanzania. My chances of meeting one of those fifty-three children from four years earlier were next to zero. I was eager to hear her story.

The girl with the pink balloon had gone to the clinic, and when it was needed, she began the ARV therapy. The medicine was working, and she was growing up as a healthy, beautiful girl. I got to play with her, to see her smile, to listen to her laugh, and I didn't even know. In that moment she became the future we hoped to create. She told me she wanted to be a pilot.

I felt amazed and grateful as the woman told me the story of the girl with the pink balloon. Finally I asked the woman, "So what's her name?" She turned to me and answered, "Her name is Jacqueline."

I believe that God gave me that moment. I expected to stand by a grave, but He wanted me to meet the other Jacqueline, who goes by Jacki. He wanted me to see the hope in her eyes and hear her sweet voice say, "Thank you."

I love God because in His kindness He speaks to His people in these ways and sustains our hearts even through our dark struggles and doubts. God gave me that moment to help redefine my expectations—we don't have to be too late.

We don't need to live in a world where children die from preventable causes. Economic poverty and all the suffering it brings can be pushed out of our world and into the history books. God has given us the mandate and every resource necessary for the task. He has made us stewards of money, knowledge, influence, and a brief amount of time on earth in which to make a difference.

A day will come when each of us steps into an unimaginable eternal life. I don't think our memories of our time on earth will be erased. And I desperately want mine to be worth remembering.

CHAPTER 5

OVERTHROWING THE TYRANNY OF LOW EXPECTATIONS

I am the Lord, the God of all mankind.
Is anything too hard for me?

—JEREMIAH 32:27

We will never be able to end poverty in this world—we live in a fallen world of much sin.

—Jennifer

End poverty? Not before Jesus returns. Man is unable to do that. The world will always have poor people.

—Bob

I don't mean to beleaguer the point, but we, as fallen man, do not have the ability to end poverty, any more than we could end sin. It's almost a little narcissistic to think that that's our calling.

—Anonymous

These comments were posted in response to a blog I wrote in October 2010, in which I claimed that it was possible to end extreme poverty. Such reactions are common to this "outrageous" statement, even among people who believe that "with God all things are possible" (Matt. 19:26).

One time I was speaking at a conference for pastors and church leaders. Before I started my speech, I asked the audience to write down the first verse that came to their minds about the poor or poverty. These pastors and church leaders clearly had an interest, if not a passion, for the poor and were taking action. But what verse on poverty and the poor do you think was most memorable to them?

"The poor you will always have with you" (Matt. 26:11a).

Hundreds of passages of Scripture to choose from, and that one topped the list. I hear someone say it almost every time I speak about the end of poverty. Why is that?

Christianity Today published an article by Tony Carnes in 2005 called, "Can We Defeat Poverty?" Three sentences into his article, Carnes writes, "Jesus said, 'The poor you will always have with you' (Matt. 26:11a). But he might also have cited corruption as another ever-present human condition."[1]

Ever-present condition.

I will offer a new perspective on this frequently misconstrued passage later in this book. For now, allow me to provoke you by declaring that Jesus did not say the poor will always be with *us*. The real issue here has to do with our low expectations.

As we've seen, expectations sit in a little control center beneath the earth of the mind. They operate the levers of interpretation and assumption that unleash or choke our hopes. When a low expectation sits on that seat and pulls those levers, he is a little tyrant closing the valves of vision, dialing down the voltage of hope, and cutting off the power of action.

If a low expectation has snuck into the control room of your thoughts, I invite you to investigate the legitimacy of his position and scrutinize the claims upon which he gained access. And as we unearth some surprising and inspiring evidence, I believe you will decide to kick that little tyrant out of the control room.

I serve as chairman of the board for an organization called Accord, North America's largest network of Christian relief and development organizations. The more than seventy participating organizations manage over five billion dollars per year to implement poverty-fighting strategies that provide clean water, microenterprises, health services, and so on. As a board, we revised the Accord vision statement to say, "Mobilizing and Equipping the Christian Community to End Poverty."

We introduced the new vision statement to the leaders of the member organizations at an assembly. One of these leaders cautiously inched his hand into the air and asked, "To end poverty?"

He hesitated and glanced around at the other leaders. He seemed to be looking for a nonverbal nudge, someone's eyes to affirm his yet unspoken perspective. I don't know what he saw, but he pressed on, "Is that really, you know, realistic?"

I'm glad he spoke up because he had the courage to ask what I'm sure was on the minds of many in the group. These people lead organizations whose mission statements aspire to exactly that goal. But there is a difference between working toward ending poverty and believing it is possible. And there is a difference between believing it is possible and expecting it to happen.

Perhaps you have that question as well, is it realistic? Maybe you share the skepticism of those who commented on the blog. You may believe ending poverty is possible in theory, but you doubt it can be accomplished in reality. After all, the statistics are overwhelming.

If you are skeptical about the possibility of ending extreme poverty, then you are not alone. In 2011 the Barna Group conducted a major survey in which 70 percent of Americans disagreed with the statement, "It is possible to end extreme poverty within 75 years."

The same survey asked, "Since 1990, do you think the percent of people in the world who are living in extreme poverty has increased, decreased, or stayed the same?" Seventy-six percent said they thought it had increased, 17 percent think it has stayed the same, and only 7 percent thought it had decreased. Similarly, about 90 percent believe the number of children dying every day from poverty-related causes is getting worse or staying the same.

"Make Poverty History." "End Poverty Now." Sounds a lot like "Save the Planet," "Save the Rainforest," "Save the Whales," and "Free Tibet." Such sloganizing is fine for raising awareness and stirring up popular engagement, but it's not to be taken seriously. These statements are shouted by frenetic activists with little nuanced understanding of the real issues. Those who believe in such slogans are naive idealists. Right?

Maybe you've experienced poverty, you've smelled it and walked in the middle of it, and because you've seen it, you're convinced the problem is too big. Ending extreme poverty isn't realistic.

We who believe in the all-powerful God have our moments of unbelief—*Sure, I believe 'with God all things are possible,' but* . . . We echo the cry of the demoniac's father, "I do believe; help my unbelief" (Mark 9:24, NASB).

And He does. Some of us are doubtful like Thomas, and He says, "Reach out your hand and put it into my side" (John 20:27). I will show you the evidence of resurrection power. I will give you the evidence you need.

Here is the astounding truth: when we look at the numbers, we see that the tyranny of extreme poverty is already being broken. The dictator is aging, and his grip on the vulnerable is weakening.

These statistics will shock you. You may wonder why you haven't seen them before:

- From 2000 to 2011, the number of kids dying from measles has declined by 71 percent (from 542,000 deaths per year to 158,000) because we are completing the work of immunizing every child.[2]
- Worldwide, between 2000 and 2012, estimated malaria mortality rates fell by 45 percent in all age groups and by 51 percent in children under 5 years of age," and most of them (3 million) were kids.[3] They did it through using insecticide-treated bed nets, accessing better medicines, and spraying to kill mosquitos. If we keep it up we will have a world free from malaria.
- We used to say that forty thousand children die each day from preventable causes. Since 1990 the global under-five mortality rate has dropped 47 percent, from 90 (89, 92) deaths per 1,000 live births in 1990 to 48 (46, 51) in 2012. And now it is down to eighteen thousand. The number of children dying before their fifth birthdays has been cut in half, and we did it in one generation using a wide range of practical strategies, from creating access to clean water to training skilled birth attendants.[4]
- Every day, there are twenty thousand *fewer* children dying of preventable causes—every day! That's remarkable progress. If we keep our current pace of progress, we will soon live in a world where massive numbers of children no longer die of preventable causes.
- In 2000 there were 102 million children of primary-school age not in school—mainly due to poverty. By 2011 that number had been cut in half, to 57 million. That's

45 million kids getting an education. Literacy rates are climbing. Those gains were made in less than ten years.[5]

- The number of HIV infections and AIDS-related deaths has fallen dramatically, according to a UN report. Death rates fell from 2.3 million during its peak in 2005 to 1.6 million last year, says UNAIDS. The number of new HIV infections fell by a third since 2001 to 2.3 million. Among children, the drop was even steeper. In 2001 there were more than half a million new infections. By 2012 the figure had halved to just over a quarter of a million. The authors contributed the fall in deaths and infection rates in children to better access to anti-retroviral drugs, which help suppress the virus.[6]

In other words, Jacki's story is not a rare exception. We are successfully protecting millions of kids from HIV infection and successfully treating more than one million more.

Until two hundred years ago, every nation on earth had an average life expectancy of about thirty years. Can you imagine if that was still true? I'd probably be dead. What if you were twenty-three years old, and the odds were you had only seven years left to live? You just spent four years getting that college degree, and now you'll have seven years to use it. That was the case for all of us a few generations ago. Except, of course, we weren't getting college degrees. Many of us weren't even literate—we were working in the fields and praying for good rain and no locusts. I'm not talking about the Stone Age here; this was life a few generations ago, until about 1800.[7]

Today, many countries have a life expectancy of close to eighty years. We have more than doubled the average length of our lives. This is not only true in prosperous countries. Throughout the world (yes, including Africa) average life spans are nearly double what they were two hundred years ago. They have increased from roughly thirty years to sixty years. The same trend is true for poverty. When we were living for only thirty years, over 90 percent of us were also living in extreme poverty. Poverty and short life spans go together.[8]

Today there are about 1.2 billion people living in extreme poverty. And that's good news. In 1981, 52 percent of the developing world's population lived in extreme poverty. Today that number is 21 percent. If we were still at 52 percent, then an additional two billion people would still be suffering in extreme poverty. We have already cut the percentage of people living in extreme poverty in half! And we did it in one generation.[9]

The voices now announcing this possibility are growing in number and credibility.

In May 2013, David Cameron, prime minister of the UK, declared, "Over a billion people still live on less than $1.25 a day. Getting to the point where no one at all is that poor is no longer a pipe dream. It can and should be one of the great achievements of our time. And it means that by 2030 everyone will have what we in Britain already consider our birthright—drinking water, electricity, healthcare and a place at school."

In April 2013, the Development Committee of the World Bank set the goal of ending extreme poverty by the year 2030. The United Nations General Assembly claimed, "Eradicating poverty in a generation is an ambitious but feasible goal." World Bank president Jim Yong Kim declared, "This is the defining moral issue of our time. Our goals are clear. End extreme poverty by 2030."[10]

In his September 2013 remarks to the UN, Bill Gates declared, "We have a special opportunity. By 2030, if we stay on track, it is reasonable to predict that we'll be very close to global equity in key categories. If we get this right, we can achieve a world in which a child from a poor country is as likely to survive and thrive as a child in a rich country."

The Brookings Institute reported, "Over a billion people worldwide live on less than $1.25 a day. But that number is falling. This has given credence to the idea that extreme poverty can be eliminated in a generation. A new study by Brookings researchers examines the prospects for ending extreme poverty by 2030 and the factors that will determine progress toward this goal."[11]

Over the past three decades, the extent of global poverty has declined rapidly. The percentage of people living in extreme poverty in 2013 is less than half of what it was in 1990. Based on this trend, it is possible to envision a world in which extreme poverty has been effectively eliminated within a generation.

It's possible, but not inevitable. It will require intelligence, wisdom, perseverance, and resources. I hear someone still insisting, "No, it will require a miracle from God." Maybe He's already done His part. Who gave us all the resources and wisdom in the first place? Maybe He's waiting for us to do what He has repeatedly told us to do.

We need to understand the engines that drove us from 52 to 21 percent, and we need to decide if those same engines are adequate to finish the task—because the final 21 percent will be difficult. But there should be no question of whether it is possible. It is absolutely possible.

The question is not, *can* we end extreme poverty? The question is, *how* can we end extreme poverty?

This book offers some perspective on that question. But before we can take that journey, the critical work of overthrowing our low expectations must be done, because the little tyrant will do everything he can to sneak back into that control room buried in your mind.

Changing expectations is hard to do. It's not like flipping a decision switch. It requires a death and resurrection.

For the first time in human history, we have the realistic possibility of ending extreme global poverty. But the presence of poverty is so historically familiar that the change is difficult to imagine. And if it is hard to imagine, it will be nearly impossible to *expect*.

Why do most people say poverty is getting worse when, as we've seen, it is rapidly getting better? Part of the answer is that most don't expect it to get better. For them, poverty is supposed to get worse, or at least to persist. Some people are so entrenched in negative expectations that they have a hard time hearing—really hearing—the above statistics. Even though the data are drawn from the most reliable global sources, we still hear what we expect to hear.

Many Christians have been trapped by low expectations for the future. Not only for the future of poverty but for the future in general. Thankfully, the old idea that the world is supposed to get worse is losing dominion. A new idea is surfacing. Maybe, just maybe, the world can get better. And maybe we will do our part to make it happen. Isn't that what Jesus prayed for? "Thy will be done on Earth."

CHAPTER 6

STAY OUT OF THE HANDBASKET

We are, all of us, never-ceasing spiritual beings with a unique eternal calling to count for good in God's great Universe.

—DALLAS WILLARD, *THE DIVINE CONSPIRACY*

To say that there are countless opportunities to heal our hurting world is nothing new. But the idea that the world could get better is itself a newborn in the minds of many Christians.

Let me unpack this a little more. We've always known that Christians should work for a better world, and many have as an expression of their faith. But it's hard to believe that it's possible to realize that better world. It's one thing to work for it but quite another to *expect* it.

Many Christians used to say, "The world's going to hell in a handbasket, and Jesus won't return until it does." This lifeboat theology says we just need to hang in there and do our best until Jesus returns. This idea assumes that things are supposed to get worse, and it feeds off of our fears of an unknown future. Twentieth-century Christians showed an insatiable appetite for devastating apocalyptic stories, which sparked best-selling books and movies.

But believing in a lifeboat theology saps a Christian's motivation to work toward a better world. It causes a fatigue of vision. In the gloom of inevitable rot, the best a Christian can do is reach out and pull a few sinking souls into the lifeboat of salvation before the flood of deterioration overwhelms the earth. How is this helpful? All you get is a bunch of tired, freaked-out Christians. Besides, what is it with hell and handbaskets? What does that even mean?

Thankfully, the tide is turning. Christians today wonder, how much better can the world get? And then the question gets personal: how can I help make it better? Our imaginations are fired by the possibility of a new earth glimpsed in Isaiah 65:17. And today's popular evangelical leaders are encouraging us to work for that future.

John Ortberg wrote in a recent article, "The Spirit wants to make you threatening to all the forces of injustice and apathy and complacency that keep our world from flourishing."[1]

The theme for Catalyst, a cutting-edge conference for the next generation of Christian leaders, in 2010 was "Unusual Tomorrow." The conference guide stated, "As catalysts, we have a responsibility to resolve issues of injustice today that make for a better tomorrow. That is our stewardship."

In 2007, Gabe Lyons launched an influential and innovative organization called Q, which convenes young Christian leaders to collaborate in shaping culture. The tagline for Q is "Ideas for the common good," and the website describes Q's purpose, "Q

was birthed out of Gabe Lyons' vision to see Christians, especially leaders, recover a vision for their historic responsibility to
renew and restore cultures. [He was] inspired by Chuck Colson's
statement, 'Christians are called to redeem entire cultures, not
just individuals.'"

Lyons, in his book *The Next Christians*, describes the promising shift from twentieth-century separatist Christians to
twenty-first-century restorative Christians—that is, Christians
who are participating with God in His great work of restoration.
He writes:

> The Christian has a calling and a responsibility to think,
> work, and live in terms of how the world ought to be in con-
> trast to reacting to how it really *is*. . . . They see injustice and
> fight it. When confronted with evil they turn it for good.
> They are motivated to bring the love of Christ into every
> broken system they encounter. Instead of being cynical and
> hopeless, they bring optimism and expectation.[2] (emphasis
> added)

Max Lucado urges, "Get ticked off. Riled up enough to respond. Righteous anger would do a world of good. Poverty is not
the lack of charity but the lack of justice . . . no one can do everything, but everyone can do something."[3]

These ideas about working for a better world are popping up
in surprising places:

> The opportunity to make [the world] better is everywhere
> if we choose to act. Better is seeing a void and filling it.
> Hearing a call for help and answering it. Taking a wrong
> and making it right. It is as small as making boots, shoes

and gear or as big as changing the world. Better is giving employees time to serve. Building a house. Painting a school. Empowering our youth. Feeding the hungry. Or revitalizing a community. Better is a call to action. A rallying cry. Fearless. Determined. Passionate. And connected. It is searching within. Reaching out. Heading into the eye of the storm. Adventuring out to the middle of nowhere. And doing so with purpose. So when the sun sets and we think about what tomorrow will bring, we understand that better is not what we do. It is who we are.

I found that message under the lid of a Timberland shoebox in 2010. Why would a shoe company spend money printing something like that? Cynics might say it is values-based brand positioning. Optimists would simply say that someone with some influence in Timberland means it and wants others to buy into it.

And this isn't just talk. Christians are living it out. Citizens of the state of Louisiana testified that in response to Hurricane Katrina, the government failed, but the church got it done. But the church didn't merely show up. It was there before Katrina, it weathered Katrina, and Jesus-followers ministered fearlessly in the aftermath.

This isn't just an American Christian phenomenon either. There is a church in Ethiopia aspiring to be their community's "beauty spot." This church cares for children in extreme poverty regardless of their faith background. They are working for a better world. One with flourishing "beauty spots."

There are hundreds of churches in Kenya that distribute insecticide-treated nets to families for protection against malaria. Many of these families never have and never will set foot inside a church. But these Kenyan Christians are working for a better world. One with less malaria.

Churches across Haiti served as distribution points for food, water, and medical services while providing counseling and prayer for the many Haitians devastated by the 2010 earthquake. They were working for a world with less post-traumatic suffering.

Around the world there are countless examples of the muscles of the good news in action. And the world is better for it.

Christians in wealthy countries are increasingly working for a better world. Many say they have a heart for the poor. But sentiment alone is insufficient. There are growing ranks of wealthy Christians who care enough about the poor and the issues of poverty to build understanding and wisdom. They want to be wise stewards of the resources God has entrusted to them. That wisdom is a critical foundation for success.

Success is not a word often used when discussing global poverty. I hope you are beginning to see that it should be.

Poverty-fighting activists tend to imagine success as a suit with a broad, insincere smile and a firm handshake. They see it as something to avoid, thinking it's probably responsible for all the suffering in the first place.

But success without pride is a good thing. It is the fruit of determination, wisdom, patience, and vision. Its attributes of professionalism and excellence are required to advance the cause of justice and end the preventable suffering caused by poverty.

Christians are no longer merely aware or concerned about the issues of global poverty and justice—they are fueling a movement of strategies to fight poverty and seek justice for the vulnerable. And chaotic movements are a good Christian tradition.

What these Christians don't realize is that they are winning the fight. They are proving wrong the cynics who say all the money trying to help Africa is throwing money down a rat hole. Turns out the world isn't a "rat hole" after all.

Does this sound like we-can-do-it triumphalism to you? It's really not. There's a solid, theological basis for this shift, which we'll explore in the next chapter.

CHAPTER 7

THE SHIFT

Prepare your minds for action.

—1 PETER 1:13 NASB

Rick Warren's book *The Purpose Driven Life* was published in 2002, selling over thirty million copies and becoming one of the best-selling books in publishing history.[1] I remember participating in devotions based on *The Purpose Driven Life* with my Kenyan brothers and sisters in our Nairobi office in 2005. It is a work of astonishing global impact. But for all its goodness, the book doesn't mention poverty. Not even once. The word *justice* appears twice, and there is one paragraph about some people speaking up for disenfranchised groups like the poor.

But, today Warren is one of the principle advocates for Christian engagement in the issues of poverty and justice. A few years after the publication of *The Purpose Driven Life*, he launched the PEACE plan—a comprehensive effort to care for Rwanda. Assistance to the poor is one of its major strategies (the A), and caring for the sick is another (the C).

What happened? Kay Warren, Rick's wife, told me about her unexpected encounter with God. She was flipping through a magazine when God grabbed her attention through an article about AIDS in Africa. She said she literally tried to cover her eyes while reading through her separated fingers because she found the images unbearable. In that moment God spoke to her, calling her to take action against what seemed to be an unconquerable global problem.

Through her, God caught her husband's attention as well, ultimately leading to a sea change at the Warrens' church, Saddleback. The church engaged not only the AIDS crisis but also other "global Goliaths" (as Rick calls them). Within a few short years, Rick Warren became a key evangelical leader in issues of global poverty.

That transition is evidence of a large-scale shift—a case study of what God is doing with His church at the dawn of the twenty-first century.

We seem to be living through a new reformation. As we saw in the previous chapter, Christians are rediscovering the call to action within their faith. We are emerging from an epoch in which the Christian faith was reduced to an intellectual position. A thing accomplished by agreement. But that one-eyed pirate of a gospel is being replaced by a fuller, richer, more demanding, and more accurate gospel.

Major segments of Christianity in the twentieth century saw a polarized gospel—half the good news. A split of the profession of faith from the demonstration of faith. We were like the son in Matthew 21:30 who said, "I will, sir" but then did not. In the last century many evangelical Christians showed a curious zeal against "works-based salvation," and the beautiful truth of "by faith alone" became a place to hide from the call to action in Matthew 25. Ephesians 2:8—"For it is by grace you have been saved, through faith—and this is not from yourselves, it is the gift of God"—was surgically excised from Ephesians 2:10—"For we are God's handiwork, created in Christ Jesus to do good works, which God prepared in advance for us to do." Concern for global poverty or social justice was dubbed a "social gospel"—the territory of dangerous liberals.

In the early part of the twentieth century, even non-Christian observers could describe the theology behind this amputation. H. G. Wells called it out in 1921. He said Christians had invented a way to gain salvation without "any serious disturbance" to their habits:

> But it is equally a fact in history that St Paul and his successors added to or imposed upon or substituted another doctrine for—as you prefer to think—the plain and profoundly revolutionary teachings of Jesus by expounding a subtle and complex theory of salvation—a salvation which could be attained very largely by formalities without any serious disturbance of the ordinary habits and occupations.[2]

We are well underway in correcting this polarization. We are healing the split. The twenty-first-century Christian will not accept a gospel in which the limbs of Christ's body on earth are amputated from the mind. The voices of reconciliation are gathering across the kingdom. If you listen you will hear a message, gentle and powerful, like the sound of an oak tree emerging from an acorn beneath the soil. A good news in muscles as well as words. A truth proclaimed *and* demonstrated.

"The reality of God's rule," Dallas Willard writes, "and all of the instrumentalities it involves, is present in action and available with and through the person of Jesus."[3] New Testament passages make plain that this kingdom is not something to be accepted now and enjoyed later, but something to be entered now (Matt. 5:20, 18:3; John 3:3, 5). It is something that already has flesh-and-blood citizens (John 18:36; Phil. 3:20) who have been transformed into it (Col. 1:13) and are fellow workers in it (Col. 4:11).

The call to this radical and life-gripping gospel is reverberating in the voices of key Christian leaders like David Platt, who writes, "Anyone wanting to proclaim the glory of Christ to the ends of the earth must consider not only how to declare the gospel verbally but also how to demonstrate the gospel visibly in a world where so many are urgently hungry."[4]

The implications of this shift are monumental. Seismic. If the forgiveness that comes by grace through faith is not an end in itself but rather a beginning, if it is a release from chains that kept us from a greater mission, and if our release from sin and engagement in God's mission are *both* part of the good news, then we Christians are an army, free and strong.

We have been saved by grace, through faith, for a reason. We have been chosen, called, redeemed, and equipped—for a reason. Ultimately, that reason is to bring God glory. Jesus made it clear that He expects us to do more than sit around and soak in His love as if it were a hot tub. Jesus' love is not a spa. His two great commands, to love God and love other people (Luke 10:27), require action. And so, the reason for our salvation, the purpose of our lives, must express itself in action to become fulfilled.

There ought to be millions of fellow workers in a position of collective power to restore the world. Not a self-generated power, but a Spirit-derived power. A God-loaned power. The power of the nobodies collectively guided and strengthened by the God who made it all and wants to buy it all back. The eternal and relentlessly loving God has given us the power of His Holy Spirit. And, though seldom acknowledged, He has also loaned us powers of imagination, social influence, wealth, and creation.

As we consider the landscape of hurts in our world, the pain caused by extreme poverty stands out as one of the greatest sources of suffering. Ending it is one of our greatest opportunities to advance the common good and God's will on earth. How then should we deploy that army, free and strong? What could we do with our God-loaned power—with our imaginations, social influences, wealth, and capacities to create?

CHAPTER 8

TRUE FAST

*If you pour yourself out for the hungry and satisfy
the desire of the afflicted, then shall your light rise in
the darkness and your gloom be as the noonday.*

—ISAIAH 58:10 ESV

Imagine a young couple in the labor and delivery room experiencing the birth of their first child. Hear her groans, see the sweat, and feel the anxious tension. Now place a bag of potato chips in the husband's hands and picture him munching away as he watches his wife give birth. As if it were on TV. It's just wrong!

Or picture a man standing in the baptismal with his pastor. He's wearing a white robe and preparing to confess Jesus as Lord of his life as he publicly identifies with the death, burial, and resurrection of his Lord in baptism. Then, out from the folds of his robe, he brings forth the bag of chips and starts munching. Never!

"Who gives this woman to be married to this man?"

"Her mother and I." Munch, munch.

No!

These are sacred moments. And in sacred moments, we do not eat. It seems wrong to eat. We don't think about not eating in the moment—it simply feels unnatural and unthinkable.

Scot McKnight defines fasting as the "natural response of a person to a grievous sacred moment."[1]

McKnight emphasizes that fasting is a natural response. Like not eating during your wedding vows because the moment is too sacred. Like not eating as you look into the casket at a funeral because the moment is too grievous.

McKnight emphasizes that fasting is a response to a very serious situation, not a device to take us from a good level to a better level.[2] Did you get that? Fasting isn't an instrument to get God to hear our prayers or to help us master a primordial impulse or to accomplish anything. It's something you do when circumstances are bad enough that you don't want to eat, and it would seem wrong to do so. Or when circumstances are incredible enough that you don't even think about food.

I am a Kansas State football fan. For decades, K-State had the worst record of any college team. Most losses, fewest wins—the losers. They were routinely trounced by other Big 8 (now Big 12) teams like Nebraska, Oklahoma, and Texas. I will never forget being at the K-State versus Nebraska game on November 14, 1998, when we, the oppressed, ignited our revolution. Nebraska held twenty-nine consecutive victories against K-State, but the stadium Jumbotron boldly declared before the game: "Today one dynasty ends. And another dynasty . . . is born."

K-State had not won against Nebraska for twenty-nine years—twenty-nine consecutive losses. So that message stirred a deep desire for vengeance. A growl in the gut. When the game clock hit 0:00 with K-State winning by a score of 40 to 30, the stadium erupted in an adrenalin-fueled roar of triumph. Everyone, myself included, could do nothing but scream, jump, and pump our arms in the air, high-fiving and hugging complete strangers as the thousands who could find their way onto the field simply ran in random directions in a continuous yelling swarm. Fans started climbing the goal post, clinging to it like ants, to bring it down (even though it was our own) in order to, what else, drag it around. It was a nearly unstoppable, bodily response to a sacred moment.

Our bodies also respond to tragic moments by natural, nearly unstoppable expressions of sorrow. My sister died when I was fifteen. When my dad told me, my mind reeled, and I was plunged into emotional turmoil. Throughout that day and for many days afterward, my parents, brothers, and I were doubled over, on our knees, pouring out unstoppable tears. I remember being on my knees, hugging myself, as I swayed with my head low to the floor. If you've ever lost a loved one or faced a terrible grief, then you understand what I'm describing. The body responds instinctively, almost uncontrollably, in grievous moments.

Whether it is as profound as the death of a sister or as trivial as winning a football game, when we feel a major experience deep in the gut, our bodies will be compelled to respond.

McKnight writes, "Sometimes we yearn so much for what we know God wants for this world, and sometimes we become so depressed over what our world is like in light of what God wants for us, that we are compelled to fast."[3]

We're living in a grievous, sacred moment.

Grievous because almost twenty-thousand children continue to die every day from preventable causes. Grievous because we give far less than 1 percent of our personal incomes to anti-poverty work. Grievous because our nation allocates only 0.17 percent of its budget to help the poor, although the average American thinks we give 20 percent.[4] Grievous because our churches spend 96 percent of their offerings on themselves[5], to pay for the facilities, staffing, and production costs of our weekly experiences. Of the 4 percent that does go beyond the church walls, only a small fraction goes to anti-poverty work. Meanwhile, the Goliath of extreme poverty is defying the army of God and slaying the innocent in the valley. Twenty-thousand every day. It feels as though we are munching potato chips while staring into the casket.

Yet this moment is also sacred. As we've shown, extreme poverty has already been cut in half. Preventable child death has been cut in half. We are witnessing a groundswell of new intentions and expectations among God's people. We have been defeated twenty-nine times in a row, but we are ready to boldly declare that today, in our generation, one dynasty ends, and a new one is born.

It is a sacred moment because our generation has the unprecedented and history-making opportunity to eradicate extreme poverty from earth. *This* is our moment. And if we feel the trembling possibilities of this moment, we won't even be able to think of munching down the chips.

When we feel in our guts what God feels when hungry children die while those who claim His name spend millions on worship centers, we will physically respond. An instinctive, nearly unstoppable action. A response driven from our alignment with God's heart. We will be compelled to drill water wells in Africa, fight government corruption, and ensure that children don't go hungry.

In February 2008, a small group of Christian leaders met in Oxford, England. They were before the Lord in prayer as they considered the seismic shifts in the world and the dramatic possibilities to make it a better place. These leaders had given their lives on behalf of the poor and oppressed, and they were seeking God's guidance for the next generation.

God drew them inexorably to Isaiah 58.

If you haven't read it recently, then read it again . . . and again. This chapter in Isaiah captures the heart of the prophet and the heart of God for the poor and oppressed. Isaiah's words about the oppressed, hungry, and poor speak to us today about people who live in slums, whose economies offer no opportunities, whose police demand bribes, who live under constant threat of gang violence, who don't have enough food to eat, who can't get clean water, and who watch their babies die of preventable causes.

In this extraordinary passage, Isaiah declares three vital messages to the religious people of his day. The passage begins with "Shout it aloud, do not hold back. Raise your voice like a trumpet" (v. 1). This is not a casual message for Isaiah to share over a cup of coffee. God demands that Isaiah proclaim this message with such power and conviction that it cannot be ignored. And what does God, through His prophet, declare?

First, God is not impressed with their religious performances. They seem eager to know God's ways—"day after day they seek me out" (v. 2)—they seem eager for God to come near, and they wonder why God hasn't noticed their fasting. But it's all wrong. Their worship is self-serving—"you do as you please" (v. 3)—produces conflict—"your fasting ends in quarreling and strife" (v. 4)—and ignores the poor.

These people seek God daily and have the appearance of righteousness, but God sees right through it, "You cannot fast as you do today and expect your voice to be heard on high" (v. 4). They are warned that they are in the presence of an unlistening God.

The second message of Isaiah 58 is that if you truly want

God's attention, if you want to please Him, and if you want your prayers to be heard, then you need to live the "True Fast"—to seek justice for the oppressed, share your resources with those in need, break the structures of oppression, honor the Sabbath, and pour yourself out for the hungry.

Verse 10 pleads, "If you spend yourselves in behalf of the hungry . . ." (NIV). Other translations read, "If you pour yourself out for the hungry" (ESV), "If you give yourself to the hungry" (NASB), and "If thou draw out thy soul to the hungry" (KJV).

This is a call to deep, personal commitment on behalf of the poor and oppressed. It must be genuine. Look again at the verbs of personal sacrifice and action—"loose the chains," "set . . . free," "share," "provide," "clothe," and "do not turn away." It is not a call to "slacktivism" or a depersonalized concern. A personal connection to the poor and oppressed is central to Isaiah 58. The prophet is showing us how to recalibrate our lives. And he's sketching out a map leading to an unimaginable treasure. A treasure of God's promises.

The promises of Isaiah 58, the third part of the message, offer assurance that if you live the True Fast then God will heal you, guard you, guide you, strengthen you, and listen to you. God will show up. You will become like a well-watered garden, like a spring whose waters never fail. You will be called "repairers" and "restorers" (v. 12). God will give you life and beauty and joy. These astonishing promises speak to the longings of His people for guidance and healing, for protection and strength, for good reputation and life. Don't we still long for these things?

The three-fold message from Isaiah 58 cries out to us today with conviction, passion, and hope. We are broken by the reprimand of our irrelevant religious performances, we are challenged to recalibrate our lives toward the True Fast, and we are struck with wonder over the incredible promises. The prophet's voice must be heard again by our generation.

Sadly we often hear only the first part of the prophet's message. Critics of our religious habits sit in the cheap seats and rant against our hypocrisy, lobbing loveless and destructive words like grenades at the church. But love for God's people motivates and saturates the prophetic words of Isaiah. Love sees what is possible and yearns for it to come alive.

Love burdens Isaiah's heart as he cries out for change. The true prophets of the twenty-first century are burdened with that same love. They don't spew their words in unguided rants. Instead, they point the way forward to greater hope and offer guidance on how to recalibrate our lives. They entice us with stories of the waiting treasure of God's promises, and they dare to share the map that will lead us to it.

The map of Isaiah 58 guides us into something that is somewhat foreign to our culture—fasting. A natural response to a grievous, sacred moment. Felt in the gut and compelling us to action. It is not simply a willingness to skip a meal. It is a change of appetite, a new desire, which motivates our actions in response to the grief and embraces the sacred opportunity.

Such action is never a show. Unlike the performances of the people Isaiah addresses, authentic action is not a notice-me religion. It doesn't try to impress people with "ta-da" charity. Instead, authentic action wants to know if it worked. Disingenuous action is pleased with itself regardless of its effect—the performance is about me, and the important thing is my act of charity. But authentic action is always motivated by something beyond itself and strives for the advancement of another. The True Fast produces a hunger that cannot be satisfied with a show—it demands results and will remain hungry until the good we desire has been achieved.

If we are serious about living the True Fast, then we will be serious about our thinking, our use of resources, and even our habits. We will create a culture of effective Christian generosity with the objective of ending extreme global poverty.

We cannot defeat Goliath by talking about him. By shouting angry words from the safety of the ridge above his valley. By posing in a posture of defiance rather than knocking him down and hacking off his head. Isaiah 58 calls us to do away with idle words. The True Fast will change us from verbal posing to authentic action—intelligent, credible, personal action rooted in love and seeking results. The end of idle words. The end of poverty.

We can fuel an unprecedented scale of social change through the church, influencing governments and even the business sector. Powered by God's love, we can charge Goliath with ferocious faith, bring him down with well-focused strategy, and hack off his head.

Our timidity here has a lot to do with our low expectations of the future. If we think the poor will always be with us, then they probably will.

It's time for new expectations. It's time to be strong.

To be effective in this fight, we have to understand our enemy. He is formidable, but we can take him. We must be released from the tyranny of our low expectations that tell us poverty is unstoppable. Similarly, we must bring clarity to the confusing claim that poverty is a metaphor rather than a brutal reality. With God-given insight into the realities, the causes, and the challenges of global poverty, we will prevail.

PART TWO

POVERTY
IS NOT AN
UNCONQUERABLE
MYSTERY

CHAPTER 9

WHY KIDS DIE

*Is it not to share your food with the hungry and
to provide the poor wanderer with shelter?*

—ISAIAH 58:7

When I was a young professor, I taught immunology and microbiology. The first lecture in microbiology class and the first chapter of most microbiology textbooks explains that microorganisms are everywhere. "They're everywhere!" It sounds like a B-movie tagline, but it's true. One especially disgusting part of that first lecture is about the fecal veneer, which means pretty much what it says.

Just about every surface we encounter is covered with bacteria, viruses, or fungi. A good portion of them travel the world via human intestines. By the end of the first day of microbiology class, each student was familiar with the oral-fecal route of the microbial world. I never surveyed the students, but I always imagined that they became more motivated to wash their hands.

I have a four-year-old son. Most dads and moms have, like

me, stood behind a little person at the bathroom sink, helping them stretch their arms up to the faucet as we explain, "After we go poo-poo we always wash our hands, okay?" With elevated tones we encourage, "Rub-rub-rub, good job, gotta make lots of bubbles to get them all clean, rinse-rinse-rinse, good, okay now dry off."

We all have our own methods of parenting and teaching kids hygiene. My way is to explain that there are little invisible monsters on their hands and that the soap bubbles trap them in little cages. When they rinse the bubbles, all the trapped little monsters go down the sink. You might think that's a bit too scary, but none of my four sons ever seemed afraid. They were fascinated and thought it was cool. I remember once when my second son, Jacob, asked, "How do the bubbles trap them?"

"Well, actually the soap doesn't trap them. It rips their skin off and makes them explode," I said. Jacob started using more soap.

Not all kids have the opportunity to wash their hands over a sink with clean water flowing out of a faucet. Over one billion people don't have access to clean water at all.

If you have kids, then you'll certainly remember those days when they were teething. How they would put anything and everything in their mouths. Whatever young children find is usually pulled in for a good gumming. The same is true of nine-month-olds around the world. Even that little person born in an impoverished slum will explore her world with her mouth.

I remember the first time I walked in a major African slum city. I was puzzled by the thousands of plastic grocery store sacks embedded in the ground. As with many poverty-stricken places, there was a lot of trash and debris, but this was the first time I saw so many little plastic baggies; I literally couldn't walk through the slum without walking on them. I asked my colleague about them.

"Flying toilets," he replied.

I thought he was joking. But I cut short a laugh as I caught the sincerity in his eyes. He said, "It's not safe to walk in the slum at night. So when someone must do their business at night, they do it in the bag and then they throw it in the alley."

In this particular slum, toilets had been flying for over twenty years. Excrement was integrated with the soil. I happened to be there on a dry day, thankfully, but rain makes the situation far worse.

I walked through that slum and saw toddlers sitting by thin streams of open sewer trickling along the edges of the alleys. They were gumming unknown objects and exploring their world of rusty bottle caps, broken glass, and flying toilets. *Where is her mom? What kind of mother would let her baby play there?* Unspoken, regrettable first reactions. Over the years, and after countless visits with people living in slum communities, I have learned the answers to questions like those.

The kind of mothers who "let their kids play there" are often dead mothers. Older sisters, elderly grandmothers, or aunties do their best to care for the highly vulnerable children of their extended families. But the most urgent issue is not the risk of infection. It is the need to eat. Those older sisters and aunties spend the day working to earn a dollar or two for food.

There are days when the older sister comes home without success. She did her best to earn some money, but she failed. She comes home to look into the eyes of her younger brothers and sisters who did not and will not eat. When the littlest ones get really hungry, they don't cry anymore.

While we childproof our houses and insert plastic caps into electrical outlets, the toddlers of the poor waddle across minefields of microbial threat.[1] Young children explore the slum worlds the same way our children explore their worlds of sanitized, soft plastics. Many children die every day as a result.

Water-borne disease is a major cause of death for children under age five. Every eight seconds, a child dies from dirty water. Yet we can celebrate because that number is far lower than in the past and is dropping rapidly. According to UNICEF, over 1.8 billion people who were without access to safe water in 1990 now have it.[2] We can hear the sound of splashing water and children at play in places that were once a dry, somber silence.

"Come, all you who are thirsty, come to the waters; and you who have no money, come, buy and eat!" (Isa. 55:1).

We have cause to celebrate, but we can't waste time because, despite our progress, nearly one billion people have not yet heard the invitation of Isaiah 55. I suggest that the best way to celebrate is to drill another well. Let's get it done.

What will it cost to finish the job? Providing clean water to every person on earth is estimated at twenty billion dollars.[3] That's a big number, but let's put it in perspective. According to the National Retail Federation, Americans spent $41,200,000,000 during the 2009 Black Friday weekend (the weekend after Thanksgiving). In a single weekend, Americans spent twice what it would cost to provide clean water to every person on earth. Which would save the lives of five thousand children every day. This is sad, good news. Sad for obvious reasons, but also good because it reveals an incredible opportunity.

Similar stories could be told for other causes of preventable child death. A vaccine to prevent measles was invented in 1963—almost fifty years ago. From 1945 to 1965, an average of four hundred thousand children per year were infected with measles in the United States, and thousands of them died or suffered mental retardation. Between 1965 and 1985, use of the vaccine dropped the cases of measles in the US by 99 percent. There were fewer than one hundred cases per year. Yet in 2008, measles still killed 164,000 children elsewhere in the world. A disease that has been preventable for almost fifty years still killed 164,000 children in 2008 simply because we failed to get the vaccine to them. And yet again, there is reason to celebrate:

> Measles deaths worldwide fell by 78 percent between 2000 and 2008, from an estimated 733,000 in 2000 to 164,000 in 2008. In addition, all regions with the exception of one, have achieved the United Nations goal of reducing measles mortality by 90 percent from 2000 to 2010, two years ahead of target. Vaccinating nearly 700 million children against measles, through large-scale immunization campaigns and increased routine immunization coverage, has prevented an estimated 4.3 million measles deaths in less than a decade.[4]

Also in 2008, malaria killed 881,000 people. Nearly all of them (85 percent) were children. Malaria is preventable with a ten-dollar net and is treatable as well. Most North Americans are surprised to learn that malaria was once endemic to the US. It is another preventable disease that can and should be eradicated. But again, there are reasons to celebrate as malaria rates are falling dramatically in response to renewed efforts.

We are on our way to defeating other major diseases, not just measles and malaria:

> Child mortality rates have fallen since 1990 in all country-income groups—with the rate of decline generally faster in high-income and middle-income countries than in low-income countries. Median child mortality fell by almost 50

percent between 1990 and 2008 in lower middle-income countries, but by only 31 percent in low-income countries.[5]

The main point is this: we should not slump in defeat before an enemy that is already halfway dead. We have proven that simple things, such as vaccines, clean water, and mosquito nets, are effective tools. We can end preventable child death. It's that simple.

In one sense poverty is simple—it's when basic human needs are not met. In another sense poverty is complex, involving damaged relationships, damaged esteem, damaged systems, and layers of injustice. Poverty is not just unmet, basic needs. It is also the injured hopes nursed by older sisters who are trying to keep their younger siblings from starvation. Where's the vaccine for damaged hope? We'll discuss that later.

To end extreme poverty we still need to understand the *why* of it. Why do such slums exist? What strategies can lift people out of those conditions or, better yet, enable people to lift themselves out? What will it take to provide clean water for everyone? What will it take to eradicate measles, malaria, and other preventable diseases? Some of these answers are simple—keep doing more of what we already know is working. But some of these answers will require new strategies.

CHAPTER 10

THE RUBBLE AND HUNGER OF POVERTY

You will be called Repairer of Broken Walls,
Restorer of Streets with Dwellings.

—ISAIAH 58:12

R ejouir worked as a messenger and driver in Haiti. He didn't make much money, but having a job with a stable income, no matter how meager, was reason to be grateful. And Rejouir was thankful for his job, but more than that, he was a grateful and proud father. His daughter had risen through the Haitian educational system with outstanding academic success. She had always dreamed of being a doctor, and now she was working to realize her dream by studying medicine.

At 4:53 p.m. on January 12, 2010, Rejouir's daughter was studying at the university when the earth began to heave. The walls swayed, and the university building she was in collapsed. She was buried in the rubble. Alive, but trapped in the darkness, she called for help.

When the massive earthquake hit Port-au-Prince, Rejouir raced to the university to find his daughter. He navigated the devastation, climbing piles of debris in an adrenaline-driven scramble through the smoke and dust. At last he came to the building where she had been studying, and he strained desperately to hear some sounds of hope.

He heard muffled voices crying out beneath the rubble, "I'm here, I'm right here, come get me."

"I'm coming," he called. "I'm coming, just hang on." He pulled away blocks of concrete and scooped out rubble with his bare hands. He clawed through chunks of cinder and scraped sandy grit away to create a path of rescue.

Rejouir dug for two days. He rescued six trapped students, but not his daughter. She died before he could get to her. She was stolen from him. His hope for the future was buried in disintegrating concrete.

I learned about Rejouir's loss as I led a medical response team in Haiti in the aftermath of that earthquake. Our team of doctors and nurses treated a twelve-year-old girl whose home had collapsed on her and pinned her hand in a cooking fire for hours. I wrestled with a wiry, seventy-year-old grandma as she writhed while we amputated her toe (despite the fact that she had plenty of anesthetic). I helped set casts and irrigate infected head injuries as the team gave medical attention to hundreds of people that week. In many cases, I prayed with the people our team treated. Yet I allowed their suffering to stay at an emotional distance I both welcomed and resented. Rejouir's story, however, could not be kept out of my heart.

Rejouir is a colleague, and hearing his story, imagining him clawing away at the concrete rubble for two days as his daughter died just a few feet away . . . well, it's unbearable. As I think about his tragedy, it stirs more than sadness or grief in me. It makes me angry.

Maybe that seems like misplaced anger. Should I get angry about an earthquake? Maybe that seems foolish, like getting angry at the weather. Not much you can do about it, right? You could shrug it off as an act of God.

Legally, an *act of God* means "events outside of human control, such as natural disasters for which no one can be held responsible." If anyone is to blame for the death of Rejouir's daughter, isn't it God?

But the suffering in Haiti was not "outside of human control" and nearly all of it was preventable. That's why I get angry. The disaster in Haiti was not an earthquake. It was a disaster of poverty. An earthquake of similar magnitude[1] struck the greater Los Angeles area in 1994, killing sixty three people. But the population of Los Angeles is *twelve times* greater than Port-au-Prince. The difference between sixty-three deaths in Los Angeles and 230,000 in Haiti is poverty. As far as I'm concerned, 99 percent of the deaths in Haiti were preventable, and poverty killed Rejouir's daughter.

Haitians were too poor to reinforce their concrete with rebar, too poor to have heavy equipment to dig people out, and too poor to provide the health care needed to treat wounds. In contrast, citizens of Los Angeles were rich enough to afford rebar, quality construction, and emergency-response capacities.

People used to think that infections and diseases were acts of God. But then we discovered antibiotics and vaccines. A lot of us are still alive today as a result. Yet there are some religious sects that refuse medical services—believing that using them demonstrates a lack of faith in God. For example, a sect in Oregon refuses medical care, and their infant mortality rate is twenty-six times higher than the general population. The state of Oregon has determined that guardians who don't allow children access to medical services can be found guilty of negligence if that child suffers or dies from preventable causes.[2] Preventable suffering and death caused by poverty should be seen in the same light.

But what is an act of God, really? Maybe the legal definition is a bit off. Should we limit God's actions to things like earthquakes and infections? We tend to credit humans with inventions like rebar and vaccines, but they're acts of God too. All good things come from Him (James 1:17). Would anyone say, "Because humans invented shoes, I won't wear them"? Because it shows a lack of faith in God? No, of course we wear them, and if we're in a right state of mind, we thank God for providing them.

Have you heard the joke about the man who was caught in a flood? He climbed onto the roof of his house and prayed, "God, save me!" A helicopter spotted him and flew over to rescue him, but he waved it off saying, "God will save me!" He continued to pray for God's rescue, and a second helicopter came which he also waved away, saying, "God will save me!" Finally the floodwaters swept him off the roof, and he died. When he arrived in heaven, the man asked God, "Why didn't you save me?" and God replied, "I sent you a couple helicopters. What else did you want?"

Antibiotics and vaccines are helicopters God sent to rescue us from the floodwaters of childhood death. Millions of children have been rescued as a result.[3] There is about a 20 percent chance that you would be dead[4] if He had not sent those discoveries. Similarly God gifted us with creativity and discovery in engineering (including simple rebar), and as a result hundreds of thousands of people did not die in the Los Angeles earthquake. When we shrug our shoulders or blame God for the deaths in

Haiti, He points to the tools and resources He placed in our hands. He may have a different view of blame.

I don't mean to oversimplify the problem of Haiti's poverty. The causes of poverty in Haiti are extremely complex, and for decades good people have worked to strengthen Haiti's development. One serious barrier to Haiti's progress is corruption. Corruption has directly and indirectly denied Haitians opportunities to thrive, much less to afford adequate building materials. And, to the detriment of the people, construction standards were ignored or bypassed with bribes. Yet even though corruption may not be entirely preventable, many democracies have shown that it is manageable.

Some natural disasters, such as earthquakes, draw a lot of attention for their suddenness and drama, but there are hundreds of disasters every year that gain little media attention. Floods and storms regularly destroy the lives and homes of the poor because of inadequate shelter. Too much water can be disastrous; too little can be just as bad. It might seem that bad weather causes famine and food shortage, but like the devastation of Haiti's earthquake, famine shouldn't be blamed on natural causes because it is preventable.

Roger Thurow and Scott Kilman, authors of *Enough*, provide important insight into the reality of food shortage and famine. They write, "For decades, the world has grown enough food to nourish everyone adequately . . . In the modern world, like never before, famine is by and large preventable. When it occurs, it represents civilization's collective failure."[5]

They provide a painfully eloquent description of the Ethiopian famine of 2003 with this conclusion, "This wasn't just a disaster scene. It was a crime scene."[6]

Thurow and Kilman describe the complicity of governments

in allowing food insecurity and famine. Governments that build the rural infrastructure needed for redistributing crops to frail markets, that set policies to ensure fair pricing, and that enable access to financing and crop insurance for farmers create stability in food supply. In other words, they prevent famine. As more governments establish appropriate policies and instruments, food production and distribution is becoming more secure, relegating famine to a dark page of human history.

Like vaccines and rebar, modern understandings of markets, transportation systems, drought-resistant seed varieties, and intelligent trade policy are all God's rescue helicopters. When He gave us the capacity to discover, to innovate, and to create, He intended for us to use those gifts for good. Nearly all the suffering caused by natural disasters is a result of inadequate shelter, and nearly all global hunger is caused by inadequate food security systems. The suffering caused by natural disasters and famine is no more unsolvable than the suffering of bare feet on a rocky path.

Poverty is a murderous tyrant killing nearly eight million children every year. We've described some of the strategies he employs in his bloodthirsty reign—measles, malaria, dirty water, hunger, HIV, and even natural disasters. The good news is that they are all solvable, and we are making rapid progress in those areas.

But if poverty were simply the visible and physical threats we've described so far, it would be easier to tackle. The truth is it has deeper, more hidden effects. To be sure, poverty is a deprivation of basic human needs, but it is also a lie. A lie whispered in the ears of those close to his breath—"You can't. Just give up." And this is the most dehumanizing effect of all. To conquer extreme poverty, we have to dispel that lie with the truth.

CHAPTER 11

POVERTY WHISPERS, "YOU CAN'T"

When he lies, he speaks his native language,
for he is a liar and the father of lies.

—JOHN 8:44

Extreme economic poverty is when you're sitting in a slum, jobless, staring at rusty bottle caps in the dirt. You wonder if you could make something out of them that other people might buy. Even for a few shillings. Then you could fill your daughter's empty stomach with some beans, and maybe have enough for yourself too. But you're so hungry now. And who would buy some rusty bottle caps, anyway? What's the point? It isn't going to get any better.

Hopelessness is the deepest trench of poverty. It cuts through the heart and mind and is very difficult to climb out of.

Imagine coming home from a fruitless search for work, hungry and fatigued, to a one-room shack with a dirt floor and a curtain for a door. Sleeping on a moldy mat that you share with your twelve-year-old daughter. Remembering the man you loved and aching over his infidelity for the thousandth time. How you and your daughter cared for him through his agonizing, HIV-induced death. You're not angry at the prostitute. You're not even angry at him. You just want him back.

After his death you couldn't afford the rent in the better part of town where you had a solid door and a concrete floor. And now you're in this hellhole. Without dinner there's nothing to do but blow out the candle, try to get comfortable on your mat, and swat the mosquitoes that might kill you. You're too tired to be afraid of them—there are things you fear more.

You fear the gangs almost as much as the police. You fear for your daughter every time she pushes through that curtain door into the violent world beyond. You wish you could find a job so you could stop borrowing rent money from your sister.

It all whispers, "It won't get any better. Just give up."

This is the disempowered state—a fatalistic outlook and condition Bryant Myers, author of *Walking with the Poor*, calls the "marred identity of the poor."[1] When you are disempowered, you shrug in defeat. You don't soldier on. You sit down and wait for a rescue that you don't expect to come. It's a condition in which you no longer hope for a better future, and you don't see yourself capable of making positive changes. Instead, you see yourself as a victim of unchangeable circumstances.

The corrupt and predatory feed on you—exploiting you with coercive power. Demanding more from you at work under threat of getting fired. Increasing your rent to include protection money for the gangs that your landlord's brother is leading. And the voices of fatalism burrow deeper into your mind:

"You can't. You're worthless."

The disempowered state is a "causequence" of poverty. There are other causequences of poverty as well: hunger, corruption, and illiteracy, among others. These simultaneously *cause* poverty and are *consequences* of it. But disempowerment is the most insidious cause of poverty and the most painful consequence. Understanding it requires insight and thoughtfulness.

To get out of the pit of hopelessness, you must climb, and yet the very strength to climb requires the hope you've lost. You must believe a better future is possible in order to strive for it. The lie whispers, "It won't get any better," and poverty wraps its coils around you when the lie is believed.

Everyone knows that a better future requires getting and keeping a job. For this, you need to strive and take risks; you need determination and hope. But when you're disempowered, your hope is beaten down, so you have no energy with which to strive. You have no faith, so you don't take risks. You can't. See the pattern? Individuals, communities, and whole nations can be trapped by the tyranny of their low expectations of themselves, their futures, and even of God.

It's difficult to rescue people from this state by giving them what they need. In fact, you might reinforce the "you can't" message. The handout can increase their sense of failure, making them more dependent on others. Therefore great wisdom is required in the work of transformational development to break the disempowered state and enable such people to regain optimism, initiative, achievement, and dignity.

The rescue strategy requires truth to combat the lie. Poverty whispers, "You can't." But God responds with encouragement such as, "With me, you can. You matter. You're loved. You're made in My image. I hear you and will walk with you on the difficult road. I have a plan, so don't give up—it *can* get better." The good news, the gospel, of Jesus Christ is a matchless, unrivaled rescue strategy in multiple dimensions.

If there is anything that exposes the lies of poverty, it is the gospel. But the proclaimed gospel is not enough. Disenfranchised people need the whole gospel—in action as well as words. They need Jesus' spoken truth, and they need His disciples to live it. They need to see the muscles of the gospel flex, expressing love in gritty, persevering, intelligent, effective action.

The good news of Jesus Christ, proclaimed and demonstrated, is the most powerful anti-poverty strategy. Jesus offers the restoration of hope, a new supportive and caring community in the church, and a strong foundation from which to try, to risk, and to succeed or fail, knowing that you'll be loved either way. The gospel leads us to love others, to forgive, to see the image of God in our enemies as in ourselves, and to discover a genuine basis for dignity and integrity. The gospel can raise a generation of men and women of integrity—servant-leaders—to displace corruption and restore social trust upon which a nation can rise. The gospel creates people who work for the Lord in the humble service of causes much bigger than themselves.

Think this is fluffy, idealistic rhetoric? It's not. I've seen it. Not just once or twice. There is an advancing wave of real people doing exactly these things, and we'll see glimpses of them in later chapters.

We don't do anti-poverty work and share the gospel. Sharing the gospel is anti-poverty work. Furthermore, it is more profound than any other effort because it penetrates layers of the human condition that cannot be reached with a vaccinating needle. The gospel brings healing and hope. It ignites new initiatives by bringing hurting people from all economic levels into relationship with God. His Holy Spirit fills us with vision, and we can see that, with God, anything, absolutely anything, is possible. Even the end of extreme poverty.

Ironically, many economically poor people believe it is possible to end extreme poverty, while the rich are pessimistic. A week after the earthquake in Haiti, I was driving through Port-au-Prince with a Haitian man, and I asked him, "Do you think it's possible to end extreme poverty?" Without hesitation he answered, "Yes," and he went on to describe why he thought poverty could end. He shared his optimism even as we drove through the rubble and past the evidence of anguish and hopelessness. A few months later, I asked the same question of a man in rural Ethiopia, a place familiar with famine and oppression, and his answer was equally quick and certain—"Yes, it is definitely possible to end poverty."

In contrast, when I have spoken about ending poverty to audiences of wealthy, American, Christian leaders, I frequently encounter skepticism. They say they're not sure that ending extreme poverty is realistic. So who's living in the disempowered state? Who's saying, "We can't. It isn't going to get better. This is just the way it is"? It's often those of us who are sitting on piles of cash and pretending the coffers are empty.

The little tyrant of low expectations is sitting in that control room beneath our minds, often justifying his position with misconstrued scripture. It's time to pull him out and strap him to a lie detector.

CHAPTER 12

THE POOR WILL NOT ALWAYS BE WITH US

Jesus said, "The poor you will always have with you"
(Matt. 26:11a). But he might also have cited corruption
as another ever-present human condition.

—TONY CARNES, *CHRISTIANITY TODAY*

Remember this statement from chapter 5? Carnes seems to be saying that there will always be kids dying from a lack of food. That's just the way it is. Like gravity. But why did he break the Matthew verse in half? What about Matthew 26:11b? More on that later.

My problem is that I've known some of those kids. After they died, I had Christians tell me that God had "called them home." But I don't believe their suffering was God's plan. It was the consequence of our sin, and God hates that sin. I'm deeply motivated by knowing those kids—they are why I'm writing this book.

Ever-present condition.

Why does our theology of poverty begin, and sometimes end, with the belief that the poor will always be with us? What does that do to our expectations?

Because this scripture is so often remembered and heavily anchors low expectations, it's critical that we look closely into the biblical story and examine the context of this incident. If Jesus really promised that the poor would always be with us, you and me, then we should abandon any hope of ending poverty because the words of Jesus are and always will be true.

The night on which Jesus spoke those words is recorded in Matthew 26, Mark 14, and John 12. It was the night Mary anointed Jesus with expensive perfume. However, to fully understand the events of that evening, it's important to begin a bit earlier on a different night in which a different woman also anointed Jesus with perfume (Luke 7).

Jesus accepted an invitation to dinner in a Pharisee's home. We can only guess at His motives for joining that dinner party, but no doubt they were rooted in love. He was relentless in mercy and often reached out to the most difficult people—the arrogant and self-righteous.

It's hard to imagine how she even got into the home, but there she was—a "woman in that town who had lived a sinful life" (Luke 7:37). A wanton reminder of the Pharisees' secret lust and thus an object of their righteous wrath. She carried an alabaster jar of perfume and a broken heart.

She approached Jesus, trembling, tears flowing from her eyes. Eyes that had seen too many men and too much hypocritical hate. Her tears dripped onto His dusty feet as she sobbed. Her hair draped across His feet as a tent for her sorrow. She began to gently brush the tears and dust from Jesus' feet with her dark strands and extended her lips to kiss them.

She cradled the alabaster jar as she wept. She had carried the slender-necked container to the Pharisee's home for this moment. She cracked open the stem, tipped the jar, and the precious liquid trickled between His toes, its passionate aroma filling the room.

What emotions did that fragrance ignite in the men who were present? What memories did such an aroma evoke? And what about the other women in the room—what thoughts and feelings were stirred within their hearts as they breathed the scent of the sinful woman?

They all watched in shock, aghast at the socially awkward scene. "If this man were a prophet, he would know who is touching him and what kind of woman she is—that she is a sinner" (v. 39). In their judgment Jesus was no prophet.

Yet Jesus accepted her love and embraced the moment to challenge the opinions of the Pharisees. A prostitute wept upon the feet of Jesus, and Jesus said to her, "Your sins are forgiven" (v. 48). He praised her for her love. He compared her actions to the stale hospitality of his Pharisee host and then summed up the comparison, "Whoever has been forgiven little loves little" (v. 47).

Perhaps Mary, the sister of Martha, was present at that dinner. If not, she certainly heard about the incident. Maybe she wondered why such a woman could be free to express her worship and adoration while she, Mary, maintained decorum. Perhaps the idea stirred in her for months afterward. She might have waited for another dinner party where she could gamble her own reputation. She might have wanted to break free of social reservations and demonstrate to Jesus that her own experience of forgiveness and love was like the prostitute's. Shortly before Jesus was executed, Mary took the opportunity to do exactly that.

It was Tuesday night, three days before the cross. Jesus and his disciples were at a dinner party thrown in His honor. This time the party was in the home of Simon the Leper, probably one of the lepers Jesus had healed (Matt. 26:6). No question, the mood was different from that of the Pharisee's dinner some months earlier. The host was a former social outcast instead of a rule-bent, image-conscious, religious leader. The party was in the town of Bethany, which is where Jesus had raised Lazarus from the dead. Lazarus was at the party and so were his sisters, Mary and Martha. (Imagine partying with a guy who had been brought back from the dead!)

Although it must have been a wonderful celebration, sorrow may have been evident in the eyes of their Lord. Jerusalem and His destiny were near, and the weight of the cross was already upon Him. His disciples and perhaps the others must have sensed this.

At her chosen moment, Mary[1], the one who preferred listening to Jesus instead of working in the kitchen with her sister, the one who watched Jesus raise her brother, Lazarus, from the dead, entered the room with an alabaster jar of perfume worth forty-five thousand dollars (a year's wages in the United States). She broke the jar and poured it on Jesus. It was a moment of true worship and adoration. The whole house filled with the smell of the perfume. Mary then bowed close to Jesus and wiped the perfume from His feet with her hair—just as the prostitute had done some months earlier.

Mary broke the rules, broke the alabaster, and risked her reputation. Jesus experienced it as worship, but He also said it was done to prepare Him for His burial. Unlike the shocked faces of the Pharisees at the previous party, the faces at this party belonged to those who loved Jesus.

Perhaps the disciples understood the profound meaning behind Mary's actions—that she was imitating the expression of love, repentance, and worship shown by another woman months earlier. They saw Mary on her knees before her Lord, hair draped across His feet and wet with perfume. The aroma that whispered what her heart might have longed to say: "I know I have been forgiven much. I'm sorry I didn't come out to meet you. That I doubted. Thank you for bringing Lazarus back. I love you."

Tears tracked through the dust of weathered faces. From the eyes that had seen His miracles. Tears from the eyes that walked out of the tomb and back into the light of life. But not everyone felt this way. In that moment of worship, someone objected, and the tender sound of worship was broken by the harsh crackling of criticism:

"Why wasn't this perfume sold and the money given to the poor? It was worth a year's wages" (John 12:5).

It was Judas Iscariot. The greedy treasurer. Judas was indignant. He looked at that liquid money dripping on the floor, its aroma filling his nose, and he got angry. I imagine Mary felt fear as she looked away from the feet of Jesus and up at her angry accuser, his eyes ablaze with righteous indignation, and might have said, "Oh, Jesus, help. Tell him it's okay."

"Why wasn't this perfume sold and the money given to the poor?" (v. 5) Judas demanded. Surely Jesus would support his cause. After all, everyone knew how important the poor were to Jesus. Judas may have mumbled his complaint to other disciples and received some sense of support before protesting because some accounts say that the "disciples" (plural) had objected. Yet John's account is clear about the identity of the agitator.

Judas glared fiercely at Mary as she knelt above the perfume-soaked feet of her Lord. Would Jesus say, "Yes, Judas, you're right. We mustn't waste our resources like this when others could use the help"?

But that's not what Jesus said. Instead He shocked Judas.

Unraveled him. Jesus saw the greed and deception in Judas's heart. Jesus knew that Judas "did not say this because he cared about the poor but because he was a thief; as keeper of the money bag, he used to help himself to what was put into it" (v. 6).

Jesus didn't affirm Judas for his good stewardship or praise him for thinking of the poor. Instead, He defended Mary, "Leave her alone . . . It was intended that she should save this perfume for the day of my burial. You will always have the poor among you, but you will not always have me" (vv. 7–8).

Matthew and Mark record that Jesus also praised and affirmed Mary, "She has done a beautiful thing to me" (Mark 14:6). Can you see Mary still at Jesus' feet gently closing her eyes in relief and gratitude, whispering thank you?

Not the response Judas expected. He was humiliated. Mary won. Judas lost. Authentic worship won. Greed lost.

But a lie was born. A fatalistic belief that has fed lethargy while many millions of children starve. We have taken Jesus' words to Judas and have used them to enshrine our anemic expectations for the world's poorest people.

In that moment, a dam broke in Judas's heart and betrayal gushed forth. The greedy treasurer turned, and the next verse in Matthew's account says Judas then went to the chief priests to sell Him out: "'What are you willing to give me if I deliver him over to you?' So they counted out for him thirty pieces of silver. From then on Judas watched for an opportunity to hand him over" (Matt. 26:15–16).

Judas had seen the miracles. He had heard the amazing teachings. Judas had just spent the evening at a party with a man who had been brought back from the dead. But something else was stirring in his heart, and this incident with Mary and the forty-five-thousand-dollar perfume spill was all he could take. Greed was Satan's tool to turn the treasurer against his rabbi. Mary's lavish worship was seen as a waste by the one who loved money more than God.

Judas agreed to sell Jesus for thirty silver coins (120 denarii). That is about one-third of the value of Mary's jar of perfume. Mary poured out a year's wages for a lavish moment of worship. Judas sold the Way, the Truth, and the Life for a third of that.

But this dinner party was to cost far more than thirty pieces of silver, or even one year's income. The unexpected cost would be paid in children's lives two thousand years later as a result of fatalistic thinking because followers of Jesus would accept a peculiar misinterpretation of His words. Such an odd interpretation that doesn't line up with any of Jesus' teachings or His actions concerning the poor.

Jesus defended Mary and confronted the greed of Judas. So why do we imagine that Jesus then stood up, spread His arms, and declared in a staged soliloquy, "Truly, truly I say to you that the Roman Empire will fall. The age of reason will come. One day a nation called America will be born, and they will discover electricity and invent vaccines. They will learn to fly, and they will put a man on the moon. They will become so wealthy and inventive that they will talk by turning their thoughts into electrical pulses that will bounce off metal in the sky. But remember this— the poor will always be with you"? And after His soliloquy, He bowed and returned to the perfume-filled moment of worship? Why do we imagine it as if He made an all-time, forevermore statement like that?

Jesus did not say the poor would always be with us. He wasn't talking to us. He wasn't talking to you. He wasn't talking to me.

When Jesus said, "The poor you will always have with you" (v. 11a), who is the "you"?

Look at it again. In all three accounts, it is *part* of a sentence. We can be certain of who He's talking to if we keep it connected to the second half of the sentence (v. 11b):

"But you will not always have me."

There it is. Jesus clearly tells us that we won't always have Him. He won't always be with us. Really? In Matthew 26, Jesus says, "You will not always have me," and in Matthew 28:20 Jesus promises, "And surely I am with you always, to the very end of the age."

So which is it? "You will not always have me" (Matt. 26:11b) or "I am with you always" (Matt. 28:20)? There won't be much debate about that. We know which one it is.

How could Jesus say both things? There is no contradiction because when Jesus spoke at that party, in that perfume-filled room, it was to Judas and maybe to the others in the room three days before His death. He told Judas and company that they would always have opportunities to help the poor, but this was one of their last chances to worship Him personally—in His physical presence.

Jesus might have beeen saying, "I'm about to die." He did not ordain endless poverty.[2]

For some this is a controversial and provocative position. Good! I want to provoke a debate because that would be healthy. It's the indifference to the question that is killing us. Did Jesus intend for the first half of His sentence to be an all-time declaration while the second half of His sentence clearly wasn't? Was Jesus quoting Deuteronomy[3] in that moment? Did Jesus declare that it is not possible to end extreme poverty?

The evidence of progress and possibility is incredibly strong. Even the agnostics and atheists are saying that it is possible to eradicate extreme poverty. Not just someday, but in our generation.

The facts behind the claim are irrefutable. Those who claim that Jesus said it is not possible better make sure they're right.

Sometimes people question whether Jesus was referring to the economically poor. They wonder if instead Jesus was speaking of the spiritually poor or socially poor—the sense in which we are all poor because poor only means sinful and broken. Yet the entire scene in question centered on the economic value of the perfume, the greed of the treasurer, and the opportunity to give money to the poor. I doubt that Judas was advocating that they should give money to the spiritually poor Pharisees. Furthermore, there are 178 instances of the word *poor* in Scripture, and the word consistently refers to a state of extreme economic insufficiency.

The use of the word *poor* as a metaphor for human brokenness or sin, rather than as an economic reality, has important consequences. It has unseen impact on our thinking and obscures the goal of ending extreme poverty. In the next chapter we expose the risks of such ambiguity and offer a clear definition of what it means to end extreme global poverty.

CHAPTER 13

WE ARE NOT ALL POOR

If any of your fellow Israelites become poor and are unable
to support themselves among you, help them as you would a
foreigner and stranger, so they can continue to live among you.

—LEVITICUS 25:35

"We went there to give, and they gave more to us than we gave to them."

"We went to be a blessing, but we were the ones who were blessed!"

Christians say these sorts of things when they return home from mission trips to impoverished countries. Maybe you've said something similar. A lot of us have, and we're certainly right. We do receive more than we give on such trips.

Roughly two million affluent Christians travel internationally each year. We often meet Christians living in poverty because the mission trips often connect travelers with a partnering indigenous church. We meet poor people who greet us with broad smiles, who welcome us warmly and call us "brother" or "sister." We meet saints.

In my experience those saints are smiling because of Jesus. Their faith is astonishing and genuine, and they know the meaning of "Man shall not live on bread alone" (Matt. 4:4) in ways that we never will.

When Christians discover saints living in poverty, they sometimes return home saying things like, "They are rich, and we are poor." Speaking metaphorically, of course, it is often true; however, using the word *poor* in that way has dangerous side-effects. Using *poor* as a metaphor dilutes its hard meaning and its scriptural meaning. In Scripture, as in the quote at the beginning of this chapter, the word *poor* means people who don't have their basic human needs met.

Even development[1] professionals are prone to the ambiguous use of the word *poor*. Some describe poverty as the "lack of shalom" or as "broken relationships," and based on these definitions, they conclude that we are all poor. But that strips the word of its power, rendering it useless, since there is then no difference between "poor human" and "human." Furthermore, if we are all poor, then by definition the poor will always be with us, and our hopes of ending poverty are in vain.

No doubt using *poor* as a metaphor is rooted in good motives, such as acknowledging our common humanity or finding a language of solidarity. Or perhaps it is used to deconstruct the power dynamics between the poor and non-poor to somehow mitigate the "god-complexes"[2] of the non-poor. Maybe development professionals favor a broad definition of poverty because it emphasizes the need for holistic strategies—healing identity, healing relationships, and empowerment. All good motives.

Whatever the motive, defining the condition of poverty as a metaphor for brokenness is a mistake with consequences.

The first problem with saying "we are all poor" is that it

allows those of us who aren't biblically poor to borrow promises meant for someone else. The many Bible passages about the poor are suddenly about us. I don't think that's our intent, but perhaps we who are wealthy Christians want to relate to (and find ourselves within) the many verses about the poor. We want to see ourselves in the story. But we should not borrow the promises of God that were meant for someone else. Wiggling our way into the place of the poor in Scripture distracts us from what God is really saying to or about other people—people who don't have enough food to eat.

If we want *poor* to mean all of us with broken relationships, then we'll need to invent a new word to describe the conditions of life (and death) endured by single moms who watch their babies die from things like diarrhea. And that word would need to replace the word *poor* in the Bible where it clearly means a state of economic insufficiency (with a few possible exceptions, such as Revelation 3:17 or the often-cited Matthew 5:3).

The second problem with such a broad definition of poverty has to do with those of us who are directly involved in the work of fighting poverty. If we are all poor, then the condition of poverty is unsolvable until Jesus returns, and anti-poverty organizations can expect to be in business for a long, long time. Perhaps those of us who work for development organizations feel that economic sufficiency is too limited a goal—it doesn't feel big enough. But lifting 1.2 billion people out of extreme poverty is a tremendous goal. And we should be working with the expectation that we will put ourselves out of business. The sooner the better.

Some organizations use the broad definition to expand the domain of their work beyond their organizational mission and competence. In fact, it can wedge the development organization entirely into the domain of the church rather than serving a segment of the church's work. The Christian development organization should focus on serving one aspect of the church's mission—helping the most vulnerable meet their basic needs. That work should be integrated with making disciples as part of the journey toward human flourishing (shalom). But development organizations should focus on the enormous task of lifting people out of economic poverty and into a state of sufficiency. The rest of the journey toward shalom, the journey we are all on, is for the church to nurture.

Third, some people argue that categorizing people into "the poor" and "the wealthy" objectifies them—they become things rather than humans. This is a semantic challenge that exists when referring to any group of people, but changing language does not remove the risk of objectifying them. If our hearts are wrong, then we will make objects of the poor regardless of what term we use. Inventing a new, non-objectifying word doesn't solve the problem. Would "economically challenged" really accomplish anything other than confusion?

Finally, and perhaps most importantly, it is disingenuous to call ourselves poor.

Imagine sitting across from that single mom who just lost her baby girl because she couldn't afford enough food. You are in her one-room shanty in the slum and the smell of open sewer fills the stagnant air. Sit on that dirt floor with her, look into her brown eyes, and tell her, "We're *all* poor."

If she is patient and kind with you (which she probably will be), then she might offer a faint smile as she averts her eyes and quietly says, "But you have food." She won't go on to point out that your food is in a refrigerator. In a home with electricity.

We are all sinners, and all of us are broken. All of us endure a "lack of shalom" and "broken relationships." All of us desire to experience the "abundant life" Jesus promises in John 10:10 (ESV). Maybe those of us with money demonstrate greater brokenness in some areas of life than those who have little money. Perhaps we have deeper infections of pride, greed, loneliness, or an anemic spiritual life. But we are not all poor. For their sake, we should use other words to describe our condition.

It's important to distinguish poverty as an economic condition with complex causes and complex consequences. Its solutions require holistic work that affects all aspects of life. But the condition itself is a lack of material sufficiency. Not all of us endure poverty's hard realities.

So I use *poverty* and *poor* to refer to extreme poverty[3] (life on less than $1.25 per day[4]—not enough to meet basic human needs). Our goal, based on that definition, is to expect the end of extreme global poverty.[5]

We are not all poor. Some of us have been entrusted with great wealth, especially those of us who have refrigerators.

PART THREE

WHAT KIND OF PEOPLE WILL END EXTREME POVERTY?

CHAPTER 14

TOM'S TRUCK

Who dares despise the day of small things?

—ZECHARIAH 4:10

A few years ago, I was invited to speak at the Center for Strategic International Studies in Washington DC on the "role of faith-based organizations in international relief and development." I was sitting in a coffee shop putting some thoughts together for the speech when my phone rang.

At that time my wife and I were having some work done on our house, and the painter, a guy named Tom, had an accident and broke the axle on his truck. Tom was grandfatherly with twinkly eyes. His truck was a beater.

My wife happened to be reading Acts chapter four that morning when she heard about Tom's truck. She immediately called me at the coffee shop and told me the story. Then she read me the passage from Acts 4:

With great power the apostles continued to testify to the

resurrection of the Lord Jesus. And God's grace was so powerfully at work in them all that there were no needy persons
among them. For from time to time those who owned land or
houses sold them, brought the money from the sales and put it
at the apostles' feet, and it was distributed to anyone who had
need. (vv. 33–35)

I thought, *That would go great in my speech!*

Then I realized she was connecting this scripture to the news
about Tom.

I had an old Jeep. A 1981 blue CJ-5 with a rebuilt straight-six.
It was super cool, even after I painted over the flames. I noticed
Tom had always admired it. (And why wouldn't he?)

After my wife read that passage, she didn't need to say anything else. I started to feel it. I'm not an emotional guy, but my
eyes got watery right there in the coffee shop as I experienced
with my wife this . . . awareness. God's Word is living and still
speaks. "Anyone who had need" (v. 35). Really? Anyone? Even
painters you hardly know?

Then I wondered self-consciously whether others in the coffee shop had noticed my tears. I had a fleeting impression that
they thought my girlfriend was breaking up with me or something. They probably wouldn't believe it if I had claimed I'd heard
the voice of God in that moment.

We gave the Jeep to Tom. I hope that doesn't sound self-glori-
fying. It wasn't worth much. I gave it away because I believe God
wanted me to. It was a small expression of world-changing power.

World-changing power.

It's not uncommon for Christ-followers to do things like
that. Acts 4:35 is still visible among His people. Two thousand
years and we're still at it. Simple generosity. Real and felt. Simple

generosity can, and probably will, end extreme global poverty if we channel it effectively.

My world-changing generosity changed Tom's life, right? Well, a week after I gave him my Jeep, he sold it and took a trip to Hawaii. I kid you not.

Does that mean my wife and I misunderstood God? I don't think so. I don't know what it means. But our faithfulness to do what we think God calls us to do sometimes takes mysterious turns that seem entirely out of whack. This kind of thing has happened a lot to Christians over the past two thousand years. We should probably be disillusioned and jaded by now. We really must be fools. But it doesn't matter. I doubt I'll show up in heaven and regret being a fool for God. I plan to keep listening and doing my best to be a faithful servant.

CHAPTER 15

THE UNCRUSHABLE MOVEMENT

You see that his faith and his actions were working together,
and his faith was made complete by what he did.

—JAMES 2:22

One day when I was in college, I was playing tennis with a friend, and I was wearing a T-shirt with some serious holes in it—one of my favorites. A poor woman in the city park happened to see me after I finished playing. She came up to me and said she had a T-shirt I could have if I wanted it. This woman was probably homeless, and it was probably her only other shirt.

She told me the Bible teaches that if you have two shirts and see someone who has none, you should give your extra shirt to him or her. I wasn't sure how to respond. This woman thought I was poor. And, motivated by her faith, she offered me her other T-shirt.

Did you catch that? A Jewish carpenter said something two thousand years ago to a group of fishermen in a backwater region of the Roman Empire. And two thousand years later, a homeless woman tries to follow His instruction by giving me her ratty, old T-shirt? That might not seem like world-changing power, but it truly is. We'll see why later.

A few years ago, an older couple gave Compassion International five million dollars. They had worked hard all their lives. They'd been frugal and wise, and their diligence had paid off—they had substantial wealth for their retirement. The American dream.

But instead of heading to the golf course, they prayed. They believed that God wanted them to give away their savings to help the poor of the world.

The husband came to visit Compassion's office. I started to thank him and tell him that his money would be managed with great integrity, when he interrupted me. "I didn't give the money to Compassion. I gave it to God." He didn't ask for a single report or update.

So when you give to the needy, do not announce it with trumpets, as the hypocrites do in the synagogues and on the streets, to be honored by others. Truly I tell you, they have received their reward in full. But when you give to the needy, do not let your left hand know what your right hand is doing, so that your giving may be in secret. Then your Father, who sees what is done in secret, will reward you. (Matt. 6:2–4)

One of my friends was a successful technology business executive. He gave five hundred thousand dollars to Compassion but insisted that his identity remain anonymous. One of my other friends lives in a home with concrete floors that he built with his own hands on the Kansas prairie. He drives a beater pickup, has six kids, and does not believe in debt. He and his wife sponsored three Compassion children despite their limited finances.

Not long ago, I was in El Salvador and met a pastor of a church. San Salvador, the capital city of El Salvador, is riddled with gang violence. Gangs rule in some barrios, and this church was in one of those—a dangerous location. The pastor told me they used to be located in a rich part of town, but God asked him to leave that area and move to the barrio to minister to gang members.

As you might imagine, there was a big debate in the church because many felt that giving and membership would decline if they moved to the barrio. People didn't want to go. But the pastor was certain about what God wanted him to do. So he did it.

Together with his wife and children, he moved into the dangerous neighborhood and began ministering to gang members. As predicted, giving and membership declined. Many people chose to go to a different church.

But the pastor earnestly ministered to the barrio gangs. He introduced me to a gang leader who had been shot and thrown in prison. Now freed, the former leader told me that when he was released, the pastor helped him get a job. The pastor befriended him, and that gang leader eventually became a Christian. He shared his new faith with other gang members and as a result many have left their lives of violence. The way of forgiveness and mercy, the way of Christ, is prevailing in a tough barrio in San Salvador because of the faith and sacrifice of a pastor.

C. T. Studd, a fifty-year-old Englishman in 1910, took the gospel to China, India, and ultimately Sudan. Studd describes his motives:

> Too long have we been waiting for one another to begin! The time for waiting is past! . . . Should such men as we fear? Before the whole world, aye, before the sleepy, luke-warm, faithless, namby-pamby Christian world, we will dare to trust

our God . . . and we will do it with His joy unspeakable sing-
ing aloud in our hearts. We will a thousand times sooner die
trusting only in our God than live trusting in man. And when
we come to this position the battle is already won, and the
end of the glorious campaign in sight. We will have the real
Holiness of God, not the sickly stuff of talk and dainty words
and pretty thoughts; we will have a Masculine Holiness, one of
daring faith and works for Jesus Christ.[1]

I think that guy definitely had the right name. Of course, this
courage and generous compassion has characterized the Christian
movement since its beginning:

With great power the apostles continued to testify to the
resurrection of the Lord Jesus. And God's grace was so powerfully at work in them all that *there were no needy persons among
them*. For from time to time those who owned land or houses
sold them, brought the money from the sales and put it at the
apostles' feet, and it was distributed to anyone who had need.
(Acts 4:33–35, emphasis added)

These words were written two thousand years ago. They
describe the dawn of a movement of people known as followers of
the Way. A people called "little Christs"—Christians.

In fact they were first called "Christians" at Antioch, a cos-
mopolitan city. The generosity of Christians from Antioch, who
sent cross-cultural financial assistance to alleviate a famine in
Jerusalem, is perhaps the first documented case of international
relief (Acts 11:28–30). The people of this new faith were motivated
to collect funds and send them to a geographically and culturally
distant place in response to the suffering there. This might seem

normal to us today, but it wasn't then. Christians made it normal, and it was one expression of a revolutionary, new way of life in the first century.

This movement is still very much alive today.

It is uncrushable. You can see it in a homeless woman offering her other shirt to a college kid because he looked needy. In a pastor moving his family away from wealth and toward danger because of the voice of God. In a couple giving their life savings to people they don't know. It has made its mark throughout modern history—in William Wilberforce and the abolition of slavery and in Christians who fought to ensure that the Universal Declaration on Human Rights was established at the founding of the UN. And it continues to be the heartbeat of many of today's great international relief and development organizations.

That two-thousand-year-old movement has outlasted every nation, every empire, and every multinational corporation. It shapes the cultures and beliefs that give rise to the representatives and policies of a nation. It was here before the US government and will endure when the US government is no more.

The Center for Strategic International Studies asked me to address the question, "What is the role of faith-based organizations in relief and development?" But a better question is, "What is the role of the government in relief and development?" We'll address that later because before we examine our government, we must understand ourselves. We have to understand who we really are. We are part of a movement with an incredible legacy that was built by God from the blood and sweat of great men, women, and children. We have the opportunity to continue that legacy today.

CHAPTER 16

THE THREAT OF LOVE

*Courage is not the absence of fear, but rather the judgment
that something else is more important than fear.*

—AMBROSE REDMOON

In the end, his body lay lifeless and unrecognizable. Mud made from dust and blood matted the pulp of flesh left clinging to his frame. God's zealous, self-righteous defenders stood unclothed and panting in a circle around him, splattered with the blood. The rush of adrenaline lingered in the veins of some who still clutched last weighty, jagged rocks. They did not relent until they were satisfied by the death of the offender. A man who served food to hungry widows and cared for the needs of their children.

Two thousand years ago Jesus launched a movement of disorganized, unfunded, powerless nobodies. No celebrities, no movers, no shakers. Yet these nobodies completely changed the world.

Historians, theologians, and sociologists can argue endlessly about how it happened, but one of the earliest recorded murders in the Christian movement illuminates the answer.

Most people in that time lived in extreme economic poverty. Their average lifespan was about thirty years. Nearly all of them were poor, but even among the poor the widows and orphans were extremely vulnerable.

The disciples clearly understood God's commands to care for the widows and orphans, that God Himself "defends the cause of the fatherless and the widow, and loves the foreigner residing among you, giving them food and clothing" (Deut. 10:18). Their scripture described why God commanded His people to give one tenth of their incomes (tithe):

> At the end of every three years, bring all the tithes of that year's produce and store it in your towns, so that the Levites (who have no allotment or inheritance of their own) and the foreigners, the fatherless and the widows who live in your towns may come and eat and be satisfied. (Deut. 14:28–29)

Jesus not only affirmed these teachings, he taught his followers to practice them with a cheerful heart. He challenged the hearts of the Pharisees by telling them that, although they were giving a tenth of their resources as commanded, they were neglecting justice, mercy, and faithfulness. Jesus said, "You should have practiced the latter, without neglecting the former" (Matt. 23:23). You should practice justice, mercy, and faithfulness without forgetting to give 10 percent of your income so that the poor and disenfranchised can eat.

Only two chapters later, in Matthew 25, we find Jesus describing the events of Judgment Day. Jesus' teachings are clear—caring for the "least of these" (v. 40) is not optional. It was commanded by God through Moses, and He hasn't changed His mind.

The early church then, as today, was a community of disciples among people with needs. The disciples noticed the widows and their desperate struggles to care for their children. A woman without a husband in that culture often had no means to provide for her basic needs. She and her children went without food, and she would be reduced to begging. She faced many other threats to her dignity, including turning to prostitution as her last option for survival unless someone demonstrated love, compassion, and generosity. This is exactly what the early church did.

They arranged a food distribution program for the widows and their kids. Then, as today, the needs strained the capacity of the church. There were ethnic conflicts and complaints of favoritism about some widows getting more food than others. The disciples found themselves investing a great deal of time and energy administering this program and felt that they were not spending enough time teaching the Word. So they decided to appoint someone to oversee the program.

Understanding this decision, and specifically the leadership qualities they found in the person selected for the work, will show how a disorganized rabble of nobodies changed the course of history. Rather than choosing someone with good accounting skills or an administrative bureaucrat, "They chose Stephen, a man full of faith and of the Holy Spirit" (Acts 6:5).

Stephen, in addition to being full of faith and the Holy Spirit, is also described as being full of grace and power. What an amazing reputation. He was a fierce contender in debate as the men who argued with him "could not stand up against the wisdom the Spirit gave him as he spoke" (v. 10). He demonstrated "great wonders and signs among the people" (v. 8). Grace. Power. Wisdom. This was a great man of God.

Think about it. Why would the disciples have chosen such a man to lead the ministry of caring for widows? They saw that ministry as vital—it was not a secondary function of the church, but important and demanding work. They knew that it took grace and the Spirit's guidance to care for the vulnerable without undermining their dignity. Wisdom to manage resources without inciting conflict. The rabble of nobodies changed the world by acting in the power of the Spirit. Their solid commitment to providing for widows and children by selecting someone like Stephen demonstrated that power.

The powerful teaching, the healing of the sick, the feeding of widows, and the demonstration of signs and wonders all combined to create a powerful result: "The number of disciples in Jerusalem increased rapidly" (v. 7). Even Jewish priests were joining this new movement. This was the power-filled church (ecclesia) that Jesus had promised to build. The church that Jesus declared would prevail against the gates of hell.

Love is a threat to the forces of hell. And hell is a fearsome opponent.

Stephen had enemies who secretly persuaded some men in the community to accuse Stephen of blasphemy. They spread lies about Stephen and stirred up the people against him. They dragged him before the Sanhedrin—the Jewish religious court—and produced false witnesses. A strategy of lies to serve the father of lies.

Stephen stood before the hostile council of the Sanhedrin. They glared at him in wrath stirred by false accusations. But there was something about him. An unexpected countenance. His face was not strained with fear and anxiety. They didn't see fear, but radiance. Not worry, but serenity. Confidence and faith.

The inquisition began. Stephen told the story of God's work among the Jewish people. He recounted God's faithfulness to guide His people despite their infidelity and resistance. Then

Stephen fearlessly spoke the truth, boldly declaring that the current trial was yet another example of the Jewish authorities resisting God.

Love stood against the gates of hell, and hell broke out in violence. With fury in their hearts, they dragged Stephen into an open space and encircled him. They didn't just roll up their sleeves for a flogging—they took off their clothes. They knew that the first few rocks would bruise and gash, but in time the rocks would hit spongy pads of inflamed flesh. Blood would splatter. A Jewish regulation taught that blood on their clothes would make them unclean and unable to partake in their ceremonies. They honored a regulation to please God while committing a murder.

Stephen's life and death embody spiritual realities. Love has enemies because it is a threat to the kingdom of darkness and violence. The father of lies who rules that kingdom might tolerate a few nice sermons and intellectual debates about truth, but he will not stand idly by when men serve food to widows in the name of Jesus. They are the point of the spear in the confrontation with hell. Such men must be targeted and destroyed.

Stephen held fast to the way of Jesus. Even with his final breath he followed his Lord's example. As sharp edges of the rocks gouged his flesh, he lost balance and fell. In that moment he cried out—not for them to stop, not with angry words. Instead he cried, "Lord, do not hold this sin against them" (Acts 7:60).

No power in hell could stop this movement of fearless love.

CHAPTER 17

FEARLESS LOVE

LORD, I have heard of your fame; I stand in awe of your deeds, LORD. Repeat them in our day, in our time make them known; in wrath remember mercy.

—HABAKKUK 3:2

Stephen's death became a catalyst for the growth of the early church. The Christians dispersed to dodge the violence of their persecutors, spreading the good news and doing good works as they fled. Some of these early Christians migrated as far as Rome.

At that time, Rome was the epicenter of human power. The Roman elite viewed the Christians with disdain—to them it was an irrelevant sect within Judaism. However, as Christians migrated into cities throughout the Roman Empire, and into Rome itself, the new faith gathered increasing recognition and membership. It seems likely that the impoverished Christian immigrants worked as servants in the estates of Rome's top citizens. There must have been something noteworthy and different about those Christian servants because they attracted the interest of their masters.

Early Roman Christians had a reputation for their concern for the poor, the sick, and the vulnerable. Just like Jesus. Just like Stephen. The early church historian, Eusebius, describes the actions of the second-century Christians when plagues struck the city:

> The most of our brethren were unsparing in their exceeding love and brotherly kindness. They held fast to each other and visited the sick fearlessly, and ministered to them continually, serving them in Christ. And they died with them most joyfully, taking the affliction of others, and drawing the sickness from their neighbors to themselves and willingly receiving their pains. And many who cared for the sick and gave strength to others died themselves having transferred to themselves their death.[1]

These Christians did not flee the sick and their dreadful infections. Instead they demonstrated "exceeding love and brotherly kindness." They ministered to the sick fearlessly and died with them joyfully. This type of love was unprecedented in the culture of Roman paganism. It was revolutionary.

Historian James Hunter explains in his book *To Change the World* that when the early church leaders declared themselves to be "lovers of the poor," they offered a new model of society. "The care of the poor emphasized a very different and more universal bond of social solidarity, namely, a common humanity."[2]

You might think that the leaders of Rome would welcome these social services. But many did not. Instead they felt threatened by the new faith and its superstitious adherents. And they tried to stamp out the movement with persecution, including public executions in which Christians were shredded and eaten by lions. The Colosseum. The threat of love again faced violence from the kingdom of darkness.

What if those second-century Christians could see us now? Those who were "exceeding in their love and kindness" during the second-century plagues—who "visited the sick fearlessly" and "died with them most joyfully." What would they have done to obtain a simple antibiotic on behalf of a sick kid today? How far would they have gone for a net to protect a child from mosquitoes infected with malaria? What if they could see us now? Perhaps they can. Perhaps they are among the "great cloud of witnesses" described in Hebrews 12:1.

God's movement persisted. The persecution did not stop the Christians from serving the poor, the sick, and the marginalized.

And Julian, the last pagan emperor of Rome, found it infuriating. He thought he was being tricked, that the Christians had invented a new strategy to secure social power by pretending to care for people. So Emperor Julian, threatened by these devious, power-hungry Christians, decided to beat them at their own game. He launched competing social services operated by the pagan priests. But competing with Christian compassion was a frustrating business. Julian wrote:

> These impious Galileans not only feed their own poor, but ours also; welcoming them into their agape, they attract them, as children are attracted, with cakes . . . Whilst the pagan priests neglect the poor, the hated Galileans devote themselves to works of charity, and by a display of false compassion have established and given effect to their pernicious errors. See their love feasts, and their tables spread for the indigent. Such

practice is common among them, and causes a contempt for
our gods.[3]

A modern translation might read, "Those d*** Christians are
tricking people into joining their stupid movement by pretending
to care about people. They're even throwing parties for the losers!" What a wonderful reputation. And so Julian, the godhead of
the most powerful empire on earth, stewed like the Grinch over
the charitable acts of impoverished migrant workers.

Thus the Christian movement flourished. Princeton sociologist Rodney Stark offers a perspective of the Christian impact on
society during this thriving season:

> Christianity revitalized life in Greco-Roman cities by provid-
> ing new norms and new kinds of social relationships able to
> cope with many urgent urban problems. To cities filled with
> the homeless and impoverished, Christianity offered charity
> as well as hope. To cities filled with newcomers and strangers,
> Christianity offered an immediate basis for attachments. To
> cities filled with orphans and widows, Christianity provided
> a new and expanded sense of family. To cities torn by violence
> and ethnic strife, Christianity offered a new basis for social
> solidarity. And to cities faced with epidemics, fires, and earth-
> quakes, Christianity offered effective nursing services.[4]

That description could easily be written today about Christianity across Africa. Christianity is helping many Africans cope with
the economic pressures driving urbanization, the brutality of poverty, and the painful realities of AIDS, malaria, and other diseases.

Christians are still caring for the orphans, the widows, and
the disenfranchised in the hardest places.

I've met pastors in India who have rescued baby girls left to die in modern acts of infanticide. I've walked the slums of Africa with Christian social workers to visit women infected with HIV as a result of their now-dead husbands' infidelity. I've witnessed the work of Asian and African Christians—doctors, nurses, lawyers, counselors, teachers, business leaders, communicators—and am inspired and humbled by their persevering services for the vulnerable. I personally know African Christian colleagues who have adopted children despite their own meager incomes. Perhaps you have also met such people.

Today there are still a lot of nobodies in the movement. Thousands of anonymous "Mother Teresas." The movement Jesus started is pressing forward. Still living the faith with fearless love.

CHAPTER 18

INCOGNITO
MOTHER TERESAS

The secret things belong to the LORD our God.

—DEUTERONOMY 29:29

I wish I could tell you the full story of a woman and her husband who served for over thirty years in a violent place. About how they provided medical services to the poor and chose to raise their children in a war-torn country. I wish you could hear her share, as I did, about her courage amidst hardship, insecurity, and persecution in the service of Jesus.

In the legacy of Stephen, her husband and his medical team were murdered for the good work they did. She shared this story with me a few months after their deaths, yet her heart remained steadfast. The uncrushable movement continues in that hard place. For that reason, and for the safety of others, she asked that her story be kept confidential.

This blank page is in honor of her untold story. And in honor of the many thousands of others like her who courageously and anonymously live out their faith. One day we will meet them, hear their stories firsthand, and praise God for their courageous faith. Perhaps your story will be one of them.

Would you use this space to write your prayer? Would you use this space to pray for them—for their safety and the success of their work? Pray also that God would use your story to continue the legacy of His unstoppable movement.

_____

_____

_____

_____

_____

_____

_____

_____

_____

_____

_____

_____

_____

_____

CHAPTER 19

WHO DO WE THINK WE ARE?

And we all, who with unveiled faces contemplate the Lord's
glory, are being transformed into his image with ever-increasing
glory, which comes from the Lord, who is the Spirit.

—2 CORINTHIANS 3:18

C hristians are like a great work of art that was lost in a garage for decades. But it's been found—a beautiful masterpiece discovered beneath a cheap, contemporary portrait.

The media[1] has slapped a cheap caricature of Christians over the masterpiece of Christian identity. The counterfeit portrays us as shallow, anti-intellectual, judgmental, disengaged, and uncool hypocrites. But we've begun peeling back the substitute work to reveal the original. The accumulation of dust and grime is being gently brushed away to reveal the brilliant lines and colors of who we really are—the beauty of our origins and the beauty of the world-changing work done by those who have gone before us.

The lords of media are fond of their image of Christianity, though it is a far cry from our Revolutionary Leader and His scrappy band of radicals. The engines of media rarely portray the truth about the scope of Christian work on behalf of the poor and vulnerable. They highlight other things. Gay Anglican priests, for example, generate weeks of saturating "news" coverage, while a Rwandan Anglican bishop serving the orphans of that country's genocide remains a nobody.

Sadly, media outlets shape our understanding of what's going on in the world. And, incredibly, they inform our perceptions of ourselves as well. We have bought the caricature and held it up as a mirror.

How we see ourselves is important because it has a lot to do with who we will become. It shapes what we expect from ourselves and determines what influence we will have on the world. As said by Walter Rauschenbusch, "As long as a man has a low conception of what a perfect human character would imply, his idea of salvation will consist in slight reforms of conduct. The higher the conception of personal or social possibilities, the larger is the task set for us."[2]

What does it mean to have a perfect human character? What would being like Jesus mean for our world? The possibilities are staggering.

I would say the church needs to hire a better PR firm. But I guess those anonymous Mother Teresas take Jesus' statement in Matthew 6 seriously, which says, "So when you give to the needy, do not announce it with trumpets, as the hypocrites do in the synagogues and on the streets, to be honored by others. Truly I tell you, they have received their reward in full" (v. 2).

Mother Teresa's organization, the Missionaries of Charity, has a policy prohibiting press and interviews. In her book *No*

Greater Love, Mother Teresa writes, "The work of moral rearmament is carried out with discretion and love. The more discrete, the more penetrating it will be."[3]

Incognito Jesus.

No doubt she was motivated by Matthew 6, and it is humble, but it must be held in tension with Jesus' other teaching in Matthew 5:15–17:

> Neither do people light a lamp and put it under a bowl. Instead they put it on its stand, and it gives light to everyone in the house. In the same way, let your light shine before others, that they may see your good deeds and glorify your Father in heaven.

This is the tension—to exist between the beautiful, spiritual practice of secret generosity and the beautiful, spiritual practice of letting your light shine that others may see your good deeds and glorify God. If we hide our lights under a bowl, we might be robbing God of glory, and yet when we let others see our good deeds, we risk cozying up with pride. On the other hand, it's possible to "let your light shine" and hardly be aware that it was your light at all, while a secret act of generosity can still be motivated by a heart filled with awful self-glory. God alone knows.

We who are Christ's ambassadors (2 Cor. 5:20) have some major challenges to overcome. Our opponent is the father of lies who wields strong power to shape public opinion about Christ and His movement. Since many of us have bought into the caricature, we fulfill our own expectations that people like us don't do amazing and cool things. Those who *are* doing them—the thousands of anonymous Mother Teresas—remain, well, anonymous. The tragic result is that we don't see ourselves as the kind of people who end extreme poverty.

Yet we are.

Don't believe the dark image projected by the media. Believe the image of Christ revealed in us, and live in the light of His truth. Look at the uncrushable movement to which you belong. The countless examples of ordinary people doing extraordinary things in the name and power of Jesus Christ.

Since the dawn of Jesus' movement until now, His kingdom continues its advance as His people align their wills to His own. We, His people, have a legacy. We have in our generation the opportunity to live in that legacy. To run our parts of the race. To bear witness once again. Alongside Stephen, alongside those who ministered to the sick in ancient Rome, alongside Wilberforce and the Clapham Circle, and alongside Dr. Martin Luther King and Mother Teresa, in the ranks of those who poured themselves out to create a river of justice in the world.

As we search for the kind of people who will bring an end to extreme poverty, we need to look no further than those who bear the name of Christ, embodying their two-thousand-year legacy, and who can do all things through Christ's strength.

That strength, His power working in us, is why we dare to hope to end poverty.

But do we understand that strength?

CHAPTER 20

STEWARDS OF POWER

Then he took his staff in his hand, chose five smooth stones from the stream, put them in the pouch of his shepherd's bag and, with his sling in his hand, approached the Philistine.

—1 SAMUEL 17:40

I try to have a time of devotion with my four boys each morning before school. One time I asked them, "Who killed Goliath?" Seems like a simple question. Many of us might answer like my seven-year-old and say, "David!" And we'd be right. Yet David claimed, "This day the LORD will deliver you into my hands" (1 Sam. 17:46) as he faced Goliath.

But David didn't sit around, waiting for the Lord to kill Goliath. David drew from his experience, declared his intentions, tried on the armor, chose the smooth stones, charged the giant, slung the rock that embedded in Goliath's forehead, and, after the takedown, drew Goliath's sword and hacked off the giant's head, which he then carried around to demonstrate what the Lord had done.

So, who killed Goliath?

As Joshua surveyed the promised land from the eastern bank of the Jordan, the Lord said, "I will give you every place where you set your foot" (Josh. 1:3). And then a great wind swept in and blew all the inhabitants of the land away, carrying Joshua and his people into the land where they settled peacefully. Or, maybe not.

What really happened after God made His promise? Joshua summoned hordes of scrappy, nomadic warriors and told them to strap on their swords. He sent spies, planned and waged violent war against the occupants of the land. Yet he, like David, declared that the Lord had given the land to them.

There were the miraculous moments—the crossing of the Jordan, the fall of Jericho's walls—but they are part of a larger story involving human tactical planning, muscle and sweat, blood and weariness.

These days we Christians are heavily advised not to do things on human effort. We are reminded that we must "let go and let God." This may be good advice to those tempted by ambition or pride . . . okay, it's good advice for all of us. But if we want to follow God and are praying for His agenda, for His kingdom to come, we'd be foolish to think it will happen without our initiative and sweat. Much is accomplished by human effort, and yet, as with David or Joshua, such actions may be seen as God's work—even by the action-takers.

The trouble is with our theology of power. We simply do not comprehend the power within us. We are quick to say that we have no power, but that's false humility. Quick to insist that it's God's power in us (and it is), but really we act like tenants claiming that the landlord should fix up the place when He has left that for us to do.

The account of the tower of Babel is an amazing story. The

story in Genesis 11 says that, "the whole world had one language and a common speech" (v. 1). Can you imagine that? Humanity was united, and they decided to build a "tower that reaches to the heavens" so they could "make a name for [them]selves" (v. 4).

I've always understood this story as God's intervention to protect humanity from the idolatry of its own achievements. And certainly that is a key point. But until recently, I had overlooked another key point.

God sees humanity building the massive tower and says, "If as one people speaking the same language they have begun to do this, then nothing they plan to do will be impossible for them" (v. 6). Nothing will be impossible for them. That is God's description of human power.

Truly we do not own this power. Like everything else, it is given to us temporarily. It's on loan. We are stewards of all that God has entrusted to us, including the power we have to make things happen.

Our power to imagine, to aspire, to plan, to influence others, to love others, to work collectively, to take action, to build, to create, to harness the wind, to extract the chemical energies of earth, to shape the future—all on loan from God.

"But we have this treasure in jars of clay to show that this all-surpassing power is from God and not from us" (2 Cor. 4:7). Somehow we often think the important point here is that we are made of clay instead of the affirmation that we contain all-surpassing power. We seem to focus on what it says about us rather than what it says about God. And ironically, we consider that focus to be the humble one.

And, as in the parable of the talents, there'll be a day in which God will ask us to report on how we used the power He entrusted to us. We'd be wise to remember that it was the guy who thought he didn't have much and buried the little he had been given who got himself into a heap of trouble. The guys who had the guts to invest, who took what they were given and put it to work, found favor.

Christians generally seem hesitant to discuss their power (especially when that word is used) because it seems to violate the image of a humble spirit. We tend to equate humility with "we are worms," and worms don't have power. Many of us build our lives on that sand foundation.

I don't remember many sermons on humility—not a popular topic, I guess—but the messages I do remember left me feeling pretty wormish. The pastor may as well have shouted, "You are worms! All of you—worms! So go be humble." It's not very motivating, nor is it true.

Compared to God, of course, we do resemble worms, and in the midst of our worst sins the real earthworms should be insulted by the comparison. Yet this view also invites a weird vanity of its own. It is still a self-focused thought. Still me thinking about me.

Pride is not a matter of saying, "I am great" or "I am not great." Pride is purely a matter of having the self at the center of one's thoughts. Whether we are thinking about ourselves as amazing and brilliant, or wretched and stupid, it is still me thinking about me. And it is pride.

C. S. Lewis, in *The Screwtape Letters*, counsels us to overlook ourselves altogether. To *forget* ourselves is true humility.[1] Humble people don't think less of themselves—they think of themselves less. But how do we do that? It's difficult to forget yourself by working really hard at it.

We need a better strategy to gain humility. And that strategy is to redirect our attention beyond ourselves to God. There are immediate and tangible ways to focus on Him, perhaps the most important being "whatever you did for one of the least of these . . ." (Matt. 25:40).

Dr. Joel Edwards offers a wonderful perspective on humility in a speech he gave at Compassion. He claims, "Biblical humility is the exercising of your power for the benefit of someone else." Edwards does not describe wormishness as the foundation of our humility. Instead he sees power as the foundation for humility.

Humility emerges when we are distracted by our love of others—when we have forgotten ourselves by occupying our thoughts and efforts on serving others, particularly on those who are hurting. On the poor and oppressed.

Humility is a by-product of love.

Remember in Isaiah 58, when the people demand, "Why have we fasted . . . and you have not seen it?" (v. 3). They were practicing their religion and wanting God to notice. They maintained a "look-at-me" religion. A religion of performances. Of self-focus. Of "ta-da" charity.

God pleaded with them to practice the True Fast—genuine worship that cares for the oppressed and vulnerable:

> Is not this the kind of fasting I have chosen: to loose the chains of injustice and untie the cords of the yoke, to set the oppressed free and break every yoke? Is it not to share your food with the hungry and to provide the poor wanderer with shelter—when you see the naked, to clothe them, and not to turn away from your own flesh and blood? (vv. 6–7)

This plea reverberates in James 1:27, "Religion that God our Father accepts as pure and faultless is this: to look after orphans and widows in their distress and to keep oneself from being polluted by the world."

Consider these statements. How do they affect your view of your potential and power?

- God created you in His own image—you resemble Him (Gen. 1:26–27).
- God knit you together and invested Himself in your formation (Ps. 139:13).
- God became a human and died on a cross to rescue you (Rom. 5:8).
- God loves you (John 3:16).
- God grants His Holy Spirit to dwell in you, to guide you, and strengthen you (John 14:26; 16:13).
- You are an "image-bearer" and an ambassador (2 Cor. 3:18; 5:20).
- You are God's masterpiece (Eph. 2:10).
- The all-powerful, all-knowing, and timeless Creator of the universe, God, has infused your being with His own Spirit and wishes to operate through you to accomplish His will at your invitation.

So much for the worm. In the light of these truths, what fears hold us back from attempting noble tasks?

For some it is fear of failure, because the noble task is always hard.

For some it is fear of looking dumb, because the noble task is always countercultural.

For some it is fear of the unknown, because the noble task is never small enough to imagine with clarity.

But the most devious fear that holds us back is the fear of pride.

The fear of pride is a significant threat to our Christian identity. It causes us to buy into the condemning narrative of "miserable sinner" spun by the lords of media and princes of this world, muting the voice that tells us we are more than conquerors. As we saw in the previous chapter, embracing the "miserable sinner" caricature explains in part why we have low expectations of ourselves and reveals our low expectations of God's redemptive power. We claim that God extracted us from the mire, but we seem to keep wallowing in it, doubting that God could really lift us to the dry, higher ground. We don't attempt great things because we don't see ourselves as the type of people who accomplish great things.

It's ironic that in attempting to be humble, we commit the greatest act of arrogance—disagreement with God. It may seem humble to say that we are nothing, but the fact is we were purchased at a great cost and endowed with power for majestic purposes. Claiming otherwise disparages God's gifts and workmanship. Affirming that we are stewards of power is only prideful if we take our eyes off of the Owner of power.

When God shows us a noble task to perform, we dare not shrink back and hide behind the false banner of humility. Moses temporarily shrank before his noble task by asking God, "Who am I?" (Ex. 3:11). It's a good question, but we tend to get pulled into it as if the question was made of gravity, and our minds get pulled into a useless orbit around it. Who am I? Miserable sinner? Ambassador of God being remade into the image of Christ? Somewhere in between?

The answer will never be found in orbit. It's more like a bike—if you stare at your bike while you ride, you'll probably fall over. Fall to the left, and you'll crash into humanism, thinking you are master of it all. But fall to the right, and you'll crash into fatalism, thinking you are a miserable worm incapable of improving yourself, much less the dirt around you. The best strategy is to get your eyes off the bike, focus forward, and pedal. Once that bike of your identity gets moving, you are less likely to fall. Get your eyes off your bike (yourself) and onto Jesus, pedal hard, and see what that identity can do. Balance will come from your velocity.

This brings us back to our central question. If the noble task is to end extreme poverty, then in which direction do we ride? Practically speaking, what will it take to deploy our God-loaned power for the good of the poor? What specific strategies can we employ to bring an end to extreme poverty?

Remember that the following strategies are not to be seen as works of man. I believe God wants us to eradicate global poverty, and He has given us the necessary resources (finances, knowledge, influence, creativity, experience, and the guidance and strength of His Holy Spirit) to do it. But we do so with constant prayer, leaning not on our own understanding (Prov. 3:5). We are praying with our sleeves rolled up as we draft a strategy and get to work.

In doing this we receive the prayer of 2 Thessalonians 1:11: "With this in mind, we constantly pray for you, that our God may count you worthy of his calling, and that by his power he may fulfill every good purpose of yours and every act prompted by your faith."

PART FOUR

THE PRIMARY COLORS OF SOCIAL CHANGE

CHAPTER 21

HOW MOM CAN END EXTREME POVERTY

For we are God's handiwork, created in Christ Jesus to do
good works, which God prepared in advance for us to do.

—EPHESIANS 2:10

W e have cross-examined the tyrant of low expectations before the jury of hopeful evidence, and he has been found guilty of obstruction of justice. We have examined ourselves and our participation in Christ's global movement, and we see that we *are* the type of people who lead massive efforts of social good. We accept that God made us stewards of His power for that purpose, and we pray that He will work through us to accomplish it. We trust in His forgiveness for when we pridefully believe we are the source of good rather than Him.

Just as David selected five stones from the stream, we, too, must have a strategy before charging against the Goliath of global poverty. Without a plan, all this talk about ending extreme poverty is idealistic rhetoric. Or worse, angry conversations held among God's people hiding in the hills above Goliath's valley.

We are stewards of power, and the One who entrusted us with that power expects us to use it well. The "works, which God prepared in advance for us to do" (Eph. 2:10) are broad in scope, including everything from lending the lawn mower to our neighbors to ending global poverty. But one of those tasks will require a more sophisticated application of our power. The power we have been loaned comes in the form of resources, knowledge, creativity, experience, influence, and most importantly, the guidance and strengthening of the Holy Spirit. We must bring all this to the table as we consider the instruments of massive social change:

> If I hope in God I must also make confident use of the natural aids which, with grace, enable me to come to Him. If He is good, and if my intelligence is His gift, then I must show my trust in His goodness by making use of my intelligence.[1]

Our strategy to end poverty requires action within the three major sectors of society. Just as all colors can be created with the right blend of red, yellow, and blue, the changes needed to end poverty can be created with the right blend of these three sectors: government, business, and the church or nonprofit (sometimes called the social sector).

Maybe it doesn't sound reasonable to expect Mom, in between soccer practice and folding laundry, to guide the poverty-fighting strategies of government, business, and the church. But not only can Mom do it, she may be the best-qualified person for the job. Let's look at each of the three sectors and consider how simple, personal actions can achieve great results.

Public Sector

The public sector of government is almost exclusively the focus of anti-poverty efforts—the activists' cries to do more for the poor often end at Capitol Hill or 10 Downing Street. Bono and the ONE campaign are well-known examples of this type of activism. They create high public visibility, raise awareness, and are credited with positive outcomes for the debt relief of impoverished countries. However, the effect of such campaigns is limited because of their narrow dependence on government policy and foreign assistance.

Government is a necessary but insufficient actor in the work to end extreme poverty. Our leaders want to make the right decisions. They want to lead a more generous nation. They would vote in favor of a 0.7 percent budget allocation to anti-poverty work (remember, it's currently only 0.17 percent of the US budget) if they truly believed their constituents would stand with them.

But our political leaders don't realize that their constituents (you and I) care deeply about the poor. Maybe they don't know that their efforts to bring an end to extreme poverty will not only demonstrate their personal nobility, it will draw forth the noble character of the American nation as well. Although the global poor do not vote in American elections, we can make their interests critically important to our government's leadership and policies.

Moms can change the future of the world by actively supporting candidates willing to work for effective generosity in the public sector. We can join them to form a new constituency for the global poor. We can "speak up for those who cannot speak for themselves, for the rights of all who are destitute" (Prov. 31:8).

Business Sector

The second sector is business. Even though anti-poverty activists tend to demonize business activities in impoverished countries as greedy, capitalist exploitations of the poor, investments are an incredibly powerful means of ending extreme poverty. A more nuanced appreciation of globalization is critical to understanding the important role of business in ending poverty. Simplistic and polarizing views of globalization and capitalism will only hinder effective anti-poverty work.

The power to leverage consumerism for social good is enormously important. Businesses may act in the interest of social good for altruistic reasons or for financial profit as they recognize that fair trade, "green" products, or other cause-associated products can add bottom-line value to the corporate ledger. When consumer purchase decisions are influenced by the promise of a better world, the forces of consumerism and capitalism can be harnessed to create it.

The products Mom purposefully buys can break the chains of oppression and release people from poverty on a massive scale. She may wield the most powerful weapon in the fight against poverty as she stands in the checkout line or clicks the buy button, but she must be protected from inane questions like "Do you want paper or plastic?" Which bag causes less ecological harm?

When facing the stress of this decision, I've sometimes imagined a Greenpeace activist jumping out from behind the counter, yelling, "Neither! You should have brought your own recyclable bags!" And I thank God that Greenpeace activists will not be deciding whether I go to heaven or hell.

Mom shouldn't have to face these decisions alone. She needs someone to figure out which corporate promises are legit, which products are truly connected to poverty-reduction, and someone to mark those products for her consideration. If we help Mom in this way, she will create a new market for the benefit of the poor.

Social Sector

The third sector is often called the social, or nonprofit, sector. It is a catchall for everything nongovernmental, such as the NGOs, or nongovernmental organizations, and nonprofits. The Church (the global body of believers) is often erroneously viewed as a subset of this sector. In fact it is a radiant force in all sectors of society. However, the local expression of the Church as congregations is part of the social sector, as are parachurch organizations (such as Compassion International). From a Christian perspective, the hundreds of thousands of local congregations and parachurch organizations are critical members of the social sector.[2]

Like our political leaders, our church leaders also want to make the right decisions. Many of them recognize the truths of Isaiah 58, and they long for their churches to demonstrate the goodness of God. Honestly, I'm not sure what barriers church leaders face as they try to lead their congregations into greater efforts for the global poor. Isaiah 58:4 mentions conflict as part of the reason God isn't pleased with the religious performances of His people ("Your fasting ends in quarreling and strife"). Perhaps the distraction of internal conflicts is a major barrier facing our church leaders.

It seems common for small, vocal posses of agenda-driven curmudgeons to embroil their church leaders in frivolous problems. Perhaps these distractions are best managed not by defense but by displacement. That seems to be the prophet's strategy in

Isaiah 58:5 when he asks, "Is this the kind of fast I have chosen?" Placing a vision of grand scope and weight at the center of the church's agenda may push the petty issues to the margin and create a unifying enthusiasm for the good news proclaimed and demonstrated.

Moms are often the ones making charitable decisions and forming the volunteer force of local churches. Moms can defend their pastors from those roving posses and affirm their leaders for guiding the church into a full gospel of word and deed. In particular, a church leader who is prioritizing the needs of the global poor will face competing (and more personally felt) needs, but Isaiah 58 assures us that the richest promises of healing, protection, guidance, and joy await those who choose the True Fast God has chosen over new carpet for the sanctuary.

So, while a new political lobby or a new fair-trade approach may be part of the solution to ending extreme poverty, the more important work is to create a new culture of effective, Christian generosity. This happens when we make poverty personal and, as individuals, take credible action for the poor. Personal, effective generosity is not only an instrument of direct anti-poverty work, it is a culture-shaping engine that can, with the right strategy, produce new markets for social good to drive the business sector and new constituencies to influence government. A growing movement of such people is already rising and generating the winds of change in all three sectors of society.

In the following chapters I will describe practical ways to shape the priorities and actions of each sector. Ways to mix the primary colors of social change that are needed to end extreme poverty. The most profound level of influence is in that ambiguous stew called culture. Our ideas, attitudes, habits, passions, hopes, and expectations simultaneously reflect and create a culture that dramatically influences the business, government, and social sectors.

So let's first find out how to create change on the cultural level, and along the way we'll touch on specific poverty-ending actions that such a culture can produce in government, business, and church or parachurch organizations.

CHAPTER 22

CREATING A GOOD NORMAL: THE ROLE OF GOVERNMENT

By defining our goal more clearly—by making it seem more manageable and less remote—we can help all people to see it, to draw hope from it, and to move irresistibly toward it.

—JOHN KENNEDY

Political leaders are like sailboat captains. They stare at the sky and poke licked fingers into it, assessing the wind to find their opinions and draw up their plans. I used to think politicians were spineless, pandering self-promoters (and some are), but now I realize that their responsiveness to the weather is good and appropriate. In fact, democracy depends on it.

Sailboat captains may have planned a route, but without a motor they must respond to the wind. It may look like they have power, but they're only harnessing the real power, which is mostly beyond their control.

Sometimes a captain may be determined to tack against the wind, but her progress will be hindered. Another captain may think it's his duty to hoist the sails and blast in whichever direction the wind blows.

The wind that fills or denies the sails of political leadership is more than mere public opinion. It's not simply determined by taking polls in shopping malls. The wind is culture—that complex mix of our aspirations, expectations, values, and habits of society. It's the stuff everyone considers normal.

Suppose for a moment that everyone in America gave 10 percent of his or her personal income to help those in need. That it was simply the normal thing to do. Imagine contemporary American politicians as kids—little Barack, Hillary, Arlen, Joey Biden, George, and Sammy—every last one of them. Imagine that they all grew up in homes where Mom and Dad gave 10 percent of their gross incomes to help people who were down on their luck, out of work, or sick without medical care. They did it because that's just what you do. Anything less would be scandalous. You'd be in the news, and your prospects for reelection would be nil.

In this scenario it's not hard to imagine what the allocation of our national budget to fight global poverty would look like. Allocating 10 percent for poverty alleviation wouldn't require lobbies, political pressure, marches, or strident activists with banners. It would flow naturally from the deeply rooted expectations and norms of our culture.

In contrast, imagine a culture in which self-interest was considered normal. A world in which someone who claimed not to act in self-interest would be viewed with suspicion. It would be a given that everyone was out for themselves. Even people whose actions seemed altruistic couldn't possibly be. Those weirdos would have to be explained away in terms of self-interest—people who volunteered in soup kitchens would say, "I find it to be a rewarding experience"; they wouldn't say, "I just like to help people." In fact, we'd be more likely to trust a person with visible, selfish motives than we would someone who seemed to be unselfish. We'd know there must be a catch. Has to be.

Just as a society that expected individuals to give 10 percent would extend that expectation to the national stage, a similar effect would be seen in a society that viewed self-interest as the root of human motivation. It wouldn't be possible to have a foreign-policy agenda based on the good of another nation. All our policies would need to be justified in terms of national interest. Even our humanitarian actions would have to be explained this way. We couldn't promote peace and security for the good of other people—it would have to be for our own sakes. We would talk about how a stable world is less likely to produce terrorists that might blow us up. Or we would describe a peaceful world as better for the businesses that prosper our economy.

This world is not hard to imagine. You might think that's how our world already is. But I believe we live in a mix of both these worlds. Consider the example of former president George W. Bush, who championed an unprecedented American response to the AIDS crisis through a highly successful program called PEPFAR, launched in 2003. Seven years later, the former president reflected upon PEPFAR in an op-ed for the *Washington Post*:

> I firmly believe it has served American interests to help prevent the collapse of portions of the African continent. But this effort has done something more: It has demonstrated American character and beliefs. America is a certain kind of country, dedicated to the inherent and equal dignity of human lives. It is this ideal—rooted in faith and our founding—that

gives purpose to our power. When we have a chance to do the right thing, we take it.[1]

If this is true, then it is powerfully important. If we are still a nation that lives out ideals rooted in faith, and if that gives purpose to our power, then the utilitarian argument of self-interest is secondary and superficial. Are we still a nation that, when given the chance to do the right thing, we take it? I believe we are.

Yet there is a competing narrative that is pervasive in our society. A narrative that claims that there are no moral absolutes, no basis for knowing what is right, and no motives more pure than those upon which we evolved (survival of the fittest). This competing narrative is producing a culture of self-interest and greed that twists good national policies into selfish ones. It's creating self-fulfilling expectations of a future of war. And it causes us to believe that it's normal for people to live in extreme poverty, ensuring that their suffering will needlessly continue. We are left expecting that some of the human population, the unfit ones, probably *should* die off.

Creating a new normal, igniting social aspirations, and reshaping expectations of the future will take Christians who "seek first his kingdom" (Matt. 6:33) and pray with our Lord for "Your will be done, on earth as it is in heaven" (v. 10). Our hopes and high expectations of the future will create new, prevailing winds that will blow the sailboats in the right direction. A culture of self-sacrifice will produce national policies of generosity.

What should we expect of our political leaders? We can't expect to create change by demanding that they sail against the wind. Superficial lobbying, marching with banners, and making phone calls to congresspeople do little to give the captains the power they need to change course. They will have influence only to the extent that such activities represent the winds of social expectation and moral courage.

The following words were written over a hundred years ago, and yet they call out to our generation with power and conviction:

> In the last resort the only hope is in the moral forces which can be summoned to the rescue. If there are statesmen, prophets and apostles who set truth and justice above selfish advancement, if their call finds a response in the great body of the people, if a new tide of religious faith and moral enthusiasm creates new standards of duty and a new capacity for self sacrifice, if the strong learn to direct their love of power to the uplifting of the people and see the highest self assertion in self sacrifice then the entrenchments of vested wrong will melt away, the stifled energy of the people will leap forward, the atrophied members of the social body will be filled with a fresh flow of blood and a regenerate nation will look with the eyes of youth across the fields of the future."[2]

Are we producing those "statesmen, prophets and apostles who set truth and justice above selfish advancement," leaders who "direct their love of power to the uplifting of the people," and who see "the highest self assertion in self sacrifice"?

A democracy offers government of the people and by the people, but not because we get to vote. We cannot vote into existence a leadership that is fundamentally different from what our culture produces. And even if we could, they would fail to create change because they are only able to lead within the realities of the climate around them. A democracy gives us back the types of people we have raised from childhood.

This is good news. Because it means that creating a culture

of effective, Christian generosity is possible. In fact, it is already growing, thanks to God's work. That culture, the culture of the True Fast, will cultivate the right kind of leaders and create the needed "response in the great body of people." You can join and nurture that growing movement in two basic ways.

First, culture is a reflection and extension of collective individual actions. If you "create a new standard of duty and a new capacity for self sacrifice," then you will not only do a lot of good but you will also inspire others to follow your example. You will help to create the new normal because the effective generosity of many individuals will produce collective generosity—including government action. Conversely, if you stand idly in the margins as this movement gathers, then your stagnation will be a burden and your inactivity will hinder the new normal. You are either in, or you are out.

Second, culture change must be generational to endure. The most powerful culture-creators are those who shape the attitudes, expectations, and actions of the next generation—moms, dads, teachers, coaches, child-ministry workers, and so on. The fact is, one of you is raising our future president, others of you are raising future senators, business leaders, pastors, and all of us are raising future consumers. That's a major opportunity. So what are you doing to raise your kids as generous agents of God's work to end poverty? You can get specific ideas for engaging kids as well as options for effective, personal action at www.compassion.com.

Before we move on to the other important sectors of society, there are legitimate questions about the effectiveness of government aid we should address.

Renowned economist Jeff Sachs, a strong advocate of government aid, argues that governments must "create an environment conducive to investments by private businesses."[3] This work is done largely by investments in infrastructure and social services to develop human capital (health and education). Sachs continues, "Governments must also maintain internal peace and safety so the safety of persons and property is not unduly threatened, maintain judicial systems that can define property rights and honestly enforce contracts, and defend the national territory to keep it safe from invasion."[4]

He argues that government aid is critical for success in ending poverty and so he champions the Millennium Development Goals (MDGs). The estimated cost of meeting the MDGs is $73 to $135 billion per year in addition to current aid. That would bring the total cost of anti-poverty aid to $135 to $195 billion per year.[5] In short, Sachs estimates that the US portion of ending poverty is only 0.5 percent of our national budget. Frankly, it's an incredibly low cost for a wealthy nation, yet one key question lingers—is Sachs right? Can government assistance get it done?

According to the African economist Dambisa Moyo, government aid has had no appreciable impact on development. Government aid does not positively impact growth or savings rates. Aid has financed unproductive public consumption rather than investment. In Moyo's scathing review of government foreign assistance, she states, "One of the most depressing aspects of the whole aid fiasco is that donors, policymakers, governments, academicians, economists and development specialists know, in their heart of hearts, that aid doesn't work, hasn't worked and won't work."[6]

I wish we could run "Sachs versus Moyo" on one of those wrestling channels to find out which economist is right.[7] But unfortunately we can't. The debate over aid effectiveness is important for Christians engaged in anti-poverty activism because nearly all campaigns—ONE, Make Poverty History, Global

Poverty Project, End Poverty Now, and many others—tend to shout the same rallying cry, "Governments must increase aid!"

If we as donor nations are simply interested in the feel-good experience of giving, then effectiveness doesn't really matter. However, if we are giving because we genuinely want to stop the preventable suffering caused by poverty, then we won't be satisfied until the effectiveness of the work is demonstrated.

Our government has already made promises to the poor when they affirmed the MDGs. But who will press our political leaders to keep their promises? It won't be the people in other countries who are struggling to survive on less than $1.25 a day. This is the chance for American Christians to speak up for those who cannot speak for themselves. "Defend the rights of the poor and needy" (Prov. 31:9).

As Christian advocates for the poor, we need intelligent guidance on how to support specific actions such as policy or foreign-aid strategy. We should fix and fund foreign assistance. Aid should be aligned to the MDGs (or similar framework for poverty reduction) and defined as those funds that provide services to impoverished people. Aid should protect and develop social, physical, and human capital, or enable a thriving business environment. Aid should also promote rule of law and legal justice for the poor.

Our leaders want to cast their votes in ways that make us a nation of effective generosity, but they claim that these issues aren't critical to their constituencies, and they even fear backlash. Let's make our support of those votes clear and strong. I think 138 million Christians can make it happen. We can create a new constituency for the global poor.

We've discussed the central importance of culture on shaping government and argued that we, collectively, create currents in which political leaders must navigate. We have also highlighted the debate over aid effectiveness at a strategic level and concluded that government is an important, but insufficient, actor in the work to end extreme poverty.

The cultural level of influence is extremely important in the other sectors (business, church, and parachurch organizations) as well. In fact our habits in those areas will have far greater impact on ending poverty than government action. You might expect the typical anti-consumerism rant in the next chapter, but you won't find it. Instead I'm calling for a new culture of consumerism that affirms the role of business in ending poverty by creating new markets for social good.

CHAPTER 23

SHOPPING FOR A BETTER WORLD: HOW BUSINESS CAN END POVERTY

To poverty can be attributed practically every destructive thing: disease, crime, and perversions of body and soul. Tackling the double-headed hydra of poverty and war is not a job for the politicians and diplomats—they have had their chance. It is a job for the organizations of the world to which the business and professional men belong. Five hundred billions of dollars toward the abolishment of poverty would be a good economic investment in the world's future welfare for it would bring peace.

—EDITORS OF *THE ROTARIAN*, JANUARY 1925

I believe that for all practical purposes we can abolish poverty. Does this sound too idealistic? Too visionary? Only if we let ourselves be tyrannized by the mistakes of the past, if we permit ourselves to be betrayed by the mistaken belief that business depressions are inevitable and that man can do nothing to change his economic destiny. I for one do not believe that,

for there is no such thing as "inevitability" for any human
phenomenon if there are enough people who oppose it.

—PAUL G. HOFFMAN, PRESIDENT OF THE
STUDEBAKER CORPORATION, MAY 1947

You may be pre-trib, you may be post-trib, you might not know the difference (or care), but one thing is certain—when Jesus returns we will be shopping. Which means I must be a post-tribber. We will shop until Armageddon. Walmart and the mall may be modern inventions, but the marketplace is not. We've been shopping from the beginning of the human economy. Beads, nuts, and furs are now plastic cards and downloads.

We have a love-hate relationship with our consumer culture. Some of us shop with stealth and efficiency, others seem to be on a romantic stroll with it, but at the end of the day, we all buy. Some of us are compulsive buyers, others with NASA-like plans; some of us with the spirit of great treasure hunters, and others with a copy of *Consumer Reports*. We ascend the mountain of products guided by Sherpas like Martha Stewart. Love it or hate it, we are consumers, and consumerism will continue to hum in the heart of our wealthy culture. Being for or against it is somewhat pointless. The real question is how to harness its power for good.

The other day a catalog from PBteen (Pottery Barn's teen-focused brand) came in the mail. (Yes, we have teens and somehow Pottery Barn found out.) Just before throwing it away, my wife noticed that the décor in their showcase teen bedrooms was accented with posters and books about saving the world. That motivated me to check out the PBteen website, where I discovered stories of "4 amazing teens—we hope their stories will move you to do something small or something huge." One of those teens, Neha, testifies that, "When I was nine I started Empower Orphans. It's a non-profit organization to help orphans in India."

TOMS shoes offers a "One for One" program promising, "With every pair you purchase, TOMS will give a pair of new shoes to a child in need." The TOMS website features a "Why we give" link that explains that their motivation is to see "A Better Tomorrow. A village of healthy, educated children have a better chance of improving the future of their entire community."[1]

There are countless examples of "cause marketing" in which for-profit companies associate marketing efforts with social or charitable causes. American businesses are rapidly increasing this type of activity from an estimated $1.11 billion in 2005 to $1.52 billion in 2008.[2] According to a recent study, 89 percent of Americans ages thirteen to twenty-five would switch from one product to a comparable product if the latter brand were associated with a "good cause."[3] Needless to say, that fact motivates companies.

One of my favorite examples of business (or its owners) advancing social good may seem improbable to some Christians. It's the story of the Guinness family and one of the world's most successful beer companies. Guinness was founded 250 years ago, and today people drink ten million pints per day. Arthur Guinness, founder of Guinness beer, was a great man of faith. He started the first Sunday schools in Ireland, fought against dueling, and chaired the board for a hospital serving the poor. In the 1890s, Rupert Guinness, future head of the brewery, received five million pounds (about $182 million today) from his father on his wedding day. Shortly after, he moved into a house in the slums and started a series of programs that served the poor.[4]

Philanthropy by businesses (or their owners) and cause marketing isn't new, but it is rapidly growing and entering new territory. Authors Matthew Bishop and Michael Green say, "As well as seeking better ways to work with charitable nonprofits, nongovernmental organizations (NGOs), philanthrocapitalists are increasingly trying to find ways of harnessing the profit motive to achieve social good."[5]

In short, some businesses and the individual entrepreneurs who lead them are bringing an investment mind-set to charity that creates new pressures for effectiveness, often focusing on job creation, human capital development (mainly health and education), and other prosperity-building activities. Some of these self-declared social-good businesses are riding a fashionable public relations trend. But either way, if they are selling us the promise of a better world, it's a good thing, and we can hold them accountable to their promise.

I remember in 1997, I walked into a Peet's Coffee and Tea in Menlo Park, California, and saw their ad for fair-trade coffee. I'd never heard of fair trade, and I figured it was just another marketing gimmick. Just another way to get me to buy stuff because it was made from 10 percent post-consumer recycled materials, was never tested on animals, and was dolphin-safe. Turns out I was wrong (not the first time). Fair trade is a big deal.

The fair-trade mark is best known for coffee and chocolate, but includes many other products. The movement started earlier than most people realize, around 1949, as an effort by Christians[6] to help producers in developing countries gain a higher price, better trade conditions, and improved sustainability. Christians? That can't be right. Hollywood assures us that we're narrow-minded, judgmental, irrelevant hypocrites. But Edna wasn't.

Edna Ruth Byler was born in 1904 and grew up in a Mennonite

community in Kansas. She was serving the Mennonite Central Committee (MCC) in 1946 when she traveled to Puerto Rico. Although Edna had known an austere life, attending a one-room schoolhouse on the Great Plains of Kansas, she was moved by the extreme poverty of Puerto Rico. Edna decided to buy handiwork from local Puerto Rican women and sell it to friends, family, and churches back home. She operated this business out of the trunk of her car and her basement until MCC made it an official part of their relief and development efforts in 1962. In 2010, my mother-in-law, Jane, a good Kansas girl herself, purchased Christmas gifts for her daughters from Edna's organization and in doing so helped artisans in Paraguay and Indonesia. Today Edna's organization is called Ten Thousand Villages and retails over twenty million dollars per year in products that help people in poor countries improve their lives.

Edna was part of the ignition for the fair-trade movement that now involves multiple networks, certification processes, and international governance. In 2008, fair-trade products accounted for a whopping $4.08 billion in sales, helping 7.5 million producers and their families.

Fair trade is not without its critics. Some economists argue that it creates "artificial price supports" and amounts to a subsidy that opposes the principles of capitalism. In short, the argument is that you should leave the market alone and let competition drive the lowest possible prices. To intervene in the market is to sin, and such interventions will ultimately fail. However, these economists seem to be overlooking an important reality in product pricing—perceptions.

Certain jeans are cool, and others are not. Between my writing this and you reading it, the most popular brands will no doubt change, but the reality of popularity will not. Products are valued today based on brand perceptions, and if we all decide that products made in Uganda are cool, but products made in France are uncool, then the price of Ugandan goods will go up, and it would be no more artificial than paying too much for, say, Abercrombie and Fitch (to choose a safely unlikeable brand). Our tastes drive demand, and I think Christians have a hankering for some economic justice. Buy fair trade, and let the supply side try to keep up with our demand.

Adam Smith, the father of capitalism, would advise us to leave the market alone on the prediction that a free market will do more good for society than our intentional work to promote social interests. He writes of the worker seeking employment, "By pursuing his own interest he frequently promotes that of the society more effectually than when he really intends to promote it."[7] Does that mean that American consumerism is a virtue? Go fat, greedy tycoons! Go shopaholics! A normal world is one that places self-interest at the center of all human motivation, right?

In fact, Adam Smith may be right, at least partially, about the free market doing more to advance social good than intentional efforts. This may be tough news for some of you to hear. Guess what is having the greatest effectiveness in reducing extreme poverty? The Happy Meal toy.

About 1.3 billion people live in China. In 1981, about 84 percent of the Chinese people lived in extreme poverty. As of 2005, that number had dropped to 16 percent. That's a 68 percent decrease in the number of people living in extreme poverty in a country of 1.3 billion people. China's improvement is a major reason for the dramatic drop in global poverty rates. How did this happen?

Enter the McDonald's Happy Meal toy, which is made where? Exactly. And so is a ton of other stuff that Americans buy—about

$296 billion[8] worth of stuff, to be specific. Ironically, the American appetite for plasticky knickknacks is breaking the back of poverty in China. Our habits at Walmart are a big part of this picture, too, because Walmart is China's seventh largest export partner, ahead of the entire country of the United Kingdom. The overseas manufacturing industries driven by American consumerism have created jobs that have increased incomes and given people the opportunity to feed their families—literally. I realize that is a horrifying statement to many.

Many would argue that we should think of the values represented by such consumerism—a throw-away culture, the environmental impact, and the joyless buying of closet-filling junk that eventually flows into garages and rented storage units. Affluenza is a disease—not a cure. And think of the way those companies exploit poor people as laborers with intolerable working conditions and pathetic pay. Not to mention the lack of safety regulations and the corner-cutting.

Yet, the fact is consumerism creates jobs that raise income levels for extremely poor people and their countries. We all have to deal with the tension created by these conflicting values. I confess that I'm not sure how to manage that tension myself and can't offer simple advice.

Incidentally, we Americans lived through the same transitions. The horrible labor conditions in developing countries are similar to the labor conditions we endured in the not-so-distant past. Imagine Oliver Twist and the industrialization in Europe as a starting point. I'm saying this not to defend such conditions but to simply put them in perspective and point out that they are transitional. Indeed such conditions are rapidly improving even today because with increased incomes and concurrent increases in the empowerment of labor, even Chinese workers are

in stronger positions to improve their labor conditions and pro-
tections. The current Chinese labor situation is perhaps similar to
the unionization movements and labor laws created in America a
few generations ago.

As for exploitation, the man who now has the dignity of
employment and income and who can feed his children may
not feel exploited. After living in extreme poverty, not having
money for food, and listening to your children cry because they
are hungry—the inner ache of sadness, the desperate prayer for
help, the sense of inadequacy or shame from not being able to
provide for the ones you love—after all that, the opportunity for
a job is a gift.

All that to say that the business sector has a lot of power to
end extreme poverty. We have briefly addressed cause-marketing
and corporate philanthropy. I place these two activities in the
same category because their essences are the same. A corporation
or its owners incur expenses associated with a social good, and
to some degree that social good is associated with a value-add to
their brand or specific products.

We have mentioned fair trade as a model for influencing business practices for the benefit of the poor. Businesses that want to
"do well at doing good" need to be rewarded for doing good. The
fair-trade concept can be leveraged in far greater ways than are
currently practiced. We can create a new market for social good
so powerful that businesses without a cause will be seen with disdain. As with political change, moms have the greatest power to
do this because women make 85 percent of America's purchasing
decisions—some people call it the "she-conomy."⁹

Our strategy to end extreme poverty must understand and
leverage the critical role of business in creating economic pros-
perity. American Christians have been made stewards of $2.5

trillion per year[10] in income, and we will go shopping with it. We can create powerful, new markets for social good focused on ending extreme poverty.

So, reward companies that demonstrate a commitment to corporate philanthropy. Reward companies that champion social causes, such as providing clean water, supporting education, combating preventable disease, fostering sustainable agriculture, and other poverty-fighting efforts. Buy fair trade. Don't worry about whether companies are using these efforts as marketing gimmicks. They *are* marketing gimmicks, and we want these gimmicks to work.

We will hold those businesses accountable, but we can't unless a few of us, hopefully a lot of us, buy their stuff based on their promise to make a better world.

Those numbers for cause-marketing ($1.5 billion) and fair trade ($4 billion dollars) may seem big, but Christian relief and development organizations operate over five billion dollars per year in anti-poverty work. Nobody knows that because, as we discussed earlier, Christians aren't supposed to be the kind of people who do incredible world-changing work. The truth is we Christians are just rolling up our sleeves—all that's going to look like a warm-up drill compared to what's coming.

CHAPTER 24

AGAINST THE GATES OF HELL: HOW THE CHURCH CAN END POVERTY

Upon this rock I will build my church, and all
the powers of hell will not conquer it.

—MATTHEW 16:18 NLT

There is one institution on earth with the capacity, the presence, the credibility, the endurance, and the passion to perform the ultimate act of caring for the poor. It is the church, the body of Christ.

The world's largest corporation is China Petro-Chemical, which boasts a labor force of 1,190,000 employees. By comparison, the church is at least a thousand times larger. The church is the only organization with hundreds of millions of members and the capacity to mobilize hundreds of millions of volunteers. I'm not just talking about the good people serving in soup kitchens—I'm talking about deployment of agents into every sector of society. Agents aligned by one Spirit and a shared hope, drawing on immeasurable riches to achieve what cannot be done alone.

Dr. Ed Green, Harvard medical anthropologist, writes of East Africa:

> Churches are found in nearly all communities in the region and wield a significant level of cultural, political, social, educational and economic influence. The Church can be viewed as the largest, most stable and most extensively dispersed non-governmental organization in any country. Churches are respected within communities and most have existing resources, structures and systems upon which to build. They possess the human, physical, technical and financial resources needed to support and implement small- and large-scale initiatives. They can undertake these actions in a very cost-effective manner, due to their ability to leverage volunteer and other resources with minimal effort.[1]

The church is unrivaled in its capacity. If you want to respond to the massive challenges of global poverty, then the church is the organization with the legs to get it done.

McDonald's is also an impressive institution. They say you can't get more than ninety miles from a McDonald's in the US. The widespread presence of the burger joint is impressive—about thirty thousand McDonald's outlets worldwide—but local churches outnumber the hamburger empire by nearly 100 to 1.

The service delivery points of local churches greatly outnumber the branches of government, as does human capacity. In some African countries, up to 70 percent of their health care is delivered by private, Christian organizations, and those services are of superior quality to government-run hospitals and clinics. We have a similar history here in the US. How many "St. Someone" hospitals are in your town?

But presence is about more than numbers. Presence must also be strategic in location. Churches exist in exactly the right locations to serve the poor. In the slums, in the villages, and in the city centers—the church is present everywhere. The church is not simply there physically either; its members are integrated within the community. Salt and light. Woven into the fabric of local society. And it has been since its earliest days.

Consider this statement written by Tertullian to describe the Christians around AD 200:

> Do we not dwell beside you, sharing your way of life, your dress, your habits and the same needs of life? We are no Brahmins or Indian gymnosophists, dwelling in the woods and exiled from life. . . . We stay beside you in this world, making use of the forum, the provision-market, and all other places of commerce. We sail with you, fight at your side, till the soil with you, and traffic with you; we likewise join our technical skills to that of others, and make our works public property for your use.[2]

The church is present not only geographically and socially but also through time as a uniquely durable, local outpost of the body of Christ. The church has outlasted every corporation, every nation, and every empire. While we envy corporations that are built to last, not one even comes close to the staying power of the church. The church was present in Rwanda before the genocide, through it, and it is still there today. The church was there before the AIDS pandemic, through it, and you can count on the church being there when that dreaded disease is finally brought to its end. Are you still skeptical? The church is the bride of Christ (Rev. 19:7–8), and she will stand with Him in eternity. If she does not defeat AIDS directly, she will certainly outlast it.

The church also has street cred. In 2006, a Gallup poll was conducted to discover which organizations Africans trusted and distrusted the most. The poll, conducted in nineteen countries, found that they were most likely to trust their churches and least likely to trust their governments. The study concluded that channeling aid through local churches may be more likely to maximize optimism among the people.[3]

Even if you were an atheist, thought the Bible was total hogwash, but wanted to effectively help the poor, you'd be a fool to overlook the church. It has the largest labor force gathered in the very locations you'd wish to reach, speaks the language, and possesses local credibility—everything necessary for effective action. Not to mention the church's strong moral commitment to integrity, honesty, and countless other virtues gained in its unprecedented track record for perseverance in such service.

Without question, the church continues to conduct important anti-poverty work, as it has since the days of Stephen. Churches support the comprehensive needs of human development, which builds human capital. Churches offer moral foundations, which build social trust, relationships, hopes, and the optimism needed for communities to overcome immense challenges. These intangibles build social and leadership capital. The church is also an instrument that shapes public thought and engagement on important issues, such as environmental stewardship, social injustices, or discrimination toward minority groups and women.

Furthermore, remember the root of poverty—the insidious

and fatalistic lie that whispers, "You can't. You don't matter, and it isn't going to get any better." What institution carries the truth that defeats that lie? Who proclaims the message that "with God you can"? Who declares, "You *do* matter and it *can* get better because God really does love us"? Who offers the only foundation of durable hope? It's the church.

But these are strategic reasons why the church plays a critical role in ending poverty. You might think I'm arguing that the church's strategic assets are its strength, but they are secondary. The ultimate reason why the church is critical to the work of ending poverty is the promise of Jesus. Jesus was given the government option and declined. Jesus could have started a business for social good, but He didn't. Instead He established the church and promised that "the gates of hell shall not prevail against it" (Matt. 16:18 KJV). The church, expressed in local, disciple-making communities, is commissioned by Jesus and empowered by the Holy Spirit to advance the kingdom on earth. And that advance includes the eradication of the evil of extreme poverty. No other organization was founded by Christ or carries the promise of victory against the forces of hell.

We have already discussed a few points in the two-thousand-year history of the church serving the poor, but we need to give special attention to developments in the twentieth century. In the 1930s, the New Deal turned a local and relational appeal for help, "Brother can ya spare a dime?", into a raft of government welfare programs and entitled attitudes. In some ways, the US government became a competitor with the church for the social role of caring for the poor. Not long after that, World War II destroyed Europe, so the US government launched major US foreign aid programs to rebuild Europe. These programs later evolved into our current federal anti-poverty programs.

Churches responded to the trends of philanthropy in the early twentieth century, to the conditions of the Great Depression, World War II, and the Korean War. As a result, the twentieth century witnessed the foundation of many non-governmental organizations (NGOs). The Catholics launched the Catholic Relief Services, the Lutherans started Lutheran World Relief, the Mennonites started the Mennonite Central Committee, the Reformed Church started the Christian Reformed World Relief Committee, and so on. Evangelicals launched World Relief as an arm of the National Association of Evangelicals, and organizations like Compassion International and World Vision were born. Most twentieth-century NGOs began as Christian organizations. But then something happened.

After Europe was rebuilt, the "aid community" began to turn its attention and budgets toward poverty alleviation. The US government needed capacity, presence, and local credibility to implement anti-poverty work in those contexts. In other words, it needed the church and, specifically, the parachurch agencies that she created. The government began offering grants to organizations that could carry out this type of work. But the money came with a catch called "separate time, separate place."

"Separate time, separate place" applies to what they call "religious instruction," and it accompanies the government's policy of funding anti-poverty work. In other words, Christian organizations can administer the vaccine or provide the antibiotic, but they are not allowed to talk about what motivates them, what truth they hold most dear, or what they believe will heal the deeper pains of poverty. If you have to talk about those things, then do it in a separate time and place. It's like telling Jesus, "By all means heal the leper, but don't say, 'follow me.'" But then again, Jesus wasn't funded by the government.

I'm not going to offer my opinion of "separate time, separate place," but I will describe its impact. Many Christian organizations saw the opportunity to do good with those government dollars, saying to themselves, "Those are my tax dollars, and I want to do some good with them!" Most of those organizations were struggling on lean budgets, so between 1950 and today many of them began receiving federal grants that required them to accommodate "separate time, separate place." By legal contract, the proclamation was to be separated from the demonstration of the good news.

Multiple forces, including government funding, conspired to advance a dualistic philosophy[4] within Christian work. These forces pressured NGOs toward secularization of their work, which had various degrees of impact on parachurch programs. Some capitulated and are today entirely secular or faith-founded, while others are still running their races well, with their eyes fixed on the Pioneer and Perfecter (Heb. 12:2). These secularizing forces are like a gravity field that pulls the Christian organizations in with money and shreds their core commitments.

Sometimes in the context of development work with the poor, there seems to be a hesitation about sharing the good news of Jesus. A spirit of Emperor Julian lingers in our midst—not only within our culture, but even within the church. As the movement of "impious Galileans" remains steadfast in its service to the poor, Julian continues to accuse us of tricking people into our stupid faith by pretending to love them. The spirit of the last pagan emperor of Rome will continue to win tragic victories if we let his accusations stick. God will judge our hearts if there is any hint of coercive power in our assistance. If we offer grace with conditions or love with qualifiers, then we do not love as Christ loves. But if we don't tell them about Jesus,[5] what will we truly accomplish?

So government funding of Christian organizations often reinforces the voice of Julian. Treat the infection, but don't tell them God cares about them. Teach the job skill, but don't pray for a job. Encourage, but make sure your portrait of hope is godless. Help, but don't say why. The government's demand for separation runs a sword through the middle of holistic, Christian work—a demonstrated and proclaimed good news. This is an extremely complex and nuanced subject, but I can summarize the situation with a simple question. Why should the bride of Christ go hat-in-hand to Uncle Sam?

For two thousand years, the church, the bride of Christ, has been the hands and feet of Christ. She has suffered bruises and she has not always maintained her focus, but the church remains His agency. This generation of Christian leaders will make a vital choice—they will either equip the church to carry out her God-given mandate, or they will see her bruised and struggling, forecasting her defeat. Will they extend their arms to lift her up, or will they turn their backs on her?

Christian organizations should not feel the pressure to turn to the government for resources to help the poor when God has given His people all the resources necessary for the work (and more). That's not to say that governments don't have an important role to play—we've already described how they do. But you can create a new center of gravity that counters the forces of secularization and dualism. You can restore and protect the work of the whole gospel.

Here's what you, one of His people, can do—support Christian, holistic ministry for the poor. American Christians can make it completely unnecessary for Christian organizations to go to Uncle Sam for support. The culture of effective, Christian generosity can reverse the trend that splits the good news in half.

Great and effective Christian agencies are punished by Uncle Sam if they talk about Jesus, but the church can reward them for it.

As Christians, would we rather have the work done in the name of Uncle Sam or in the name of Jesus Christ? Whom do we want to glorify? Ask questions of the organizations you support. Ask them to describe their commitment to the whole gospel—to both word and deed.

PART FIVE

CATALYSTS AND STRATEGY

CHAPTER 25

FAST LIVING

When you fast, do not be like the hypocrites.

—JESUS (MATTHEW 6:16 NKJV)

The end of extreme poverty will require deep social resolve. Guiding the three sectors of society (government, business, and church) depends on our collective will and culture-shaping currents. God wants to put an end to the preventable suffering and death caused by extreme poverty. The question is, what do we want? How bad do we want it?

Some decisions are made in the soul—in the core of our beings. What causes a soul to decide that the status quo is intolerable, compelling it to embark on a journey to ease its pain even when the road is uncertain and the destination is hard to imagine? Hunger.

The desires of the heart are hunger pains that drive our actions. The psalmist writes, "Take delight in the LORD, and he will give you the desires of your heart" (Ps. 37:4). Jesus didn't come to make sure we wouldn't be hungry—He came to make sure we were hungry for the right things. When we abide in Christ, our desires are reoriented to align with His.

God uses life's hard experiences to snap us out of our self-satisfied world. He puts us at a graveside and shows us the number of our days. He has us on our knees in the dirt of Tanzania to be with a girl during her final day on earth. He shows us painful things and, if we're close to Him, we're drawn into His desires to heal the world.

Walking with Jesus doesn't diminish the soul's hunger, it increases it a thousand-fold. As you are drawn into His desires, you find profound joy and purpose, but you also encounter an unbearable, compulsive force. Jesus feels what the poor feel. He has solidarity with their suffering. If we dare to abide in Him, then the intensity of His love for the poor will infuse our own souls. And it will cost us.

When the extreme poverty endured by others feels like a threat to our own dignity, the desire for change rumbles in our stomachs and burns "like a fire, a fire shut up in [our] bones" (Jer. 20:9). Ordinary things may become difficult.

It may disturb your sleep, and you'll find yourself praying at 2 a.m. It may discover you seated in front of a nice meal, and you'll feel like you can't eat it. It may cause you to walk away from a well-built and prosperous career. It may put you on airplanes to destinations you cannot pronounce.

While on that journey, you discover that the pain not only can be alleviated but that its source can be eradicated. When your eyes are opened to possibilities only a few others seem to see, you'll find yourself pleading with every neighbor and friend, "Wake up! Wake up!" to show them what's happening on the horizon.

Isaiah's call to "Shout it aloud, do not hold back. Raise your voice like a trumpet. Declare . . ." (Isa. 58:1) will be God speaking to you.

With every Christian who responds to that call, with each one who rises out of the spiritual grogginess and into new expectations, God's work gathers momentum. A groundswell of collective will to which governments and markets inevitably respond. When we want it in our bones, there will be no calming our impatient and revolutionary intentions.

We are witnessing that awakening. But the shout is not enough. Like flopping a sleepy hand onto the Snooze button, we're at risk of muting the shout. Until we swing our feet out of bed and take action, we risk oversleeping the alarm. And getting out of bed requires a willingness to become uncomfortable.

The blankets of apathy and familiar thinking are warm and comforting. It will take an intentional act to throw them off to get ready for the day. But it is out there in the uncomfortable elements that the vigor, adventure, purpose, and joy of life await. If we intend to journey with Jesus, we'd better listen to what the guide says about the road ahead—"Foxes have dens and birds have nests, but the Son of Man has no place to lay his head" (Matt. 8:20).

The shout is not enough—Isaiah calls us forward into action. The fast must be chosen. How do you make yourself hungry? Don't eat. That's not an easy thing to do, but two things make it easier. First, the fast is never about the food you aren't eating—it's about the *reason* you aren't eating it. Second, it's easier to fast within a community of committed friends.

In describing the biblical foundation and purposes behind fasting, McKnight writes, "The first companion of fasting is to give to the poor, or more generally to pursue justice."[1] The connection between fasting and acts of compassion has been strong in

Christian practice since the beginning of the movement. An early Christian writing, *The Shepherd of Hermas*, advises Christians, "Estimate the cost of the food you would have eaten on that day and give that amount to a widow or orphan or someone in need." Augustine counsels, "Your distress will profit you if you afford comfort to others."[2]

The concept of going hungry can extend well beyond food. But moving from platitudes into practice is where it all becomes real and annoyingly practical.

When I didn't play golf, I thought it was the stupidest game. Now that I do play, I can verify it. For whatever reason among medical-types, the invitations to play golf are never ending. After dodging a number of those invitations, I finally gave in. A friend assured me that this particular tournament was a "best ball" tournament and that I could therefore whack my golf ball into the woods, weeds, and lakes on every stroke, and it wouldn't matter.

"All you have to do is ride around in a cart and drink beer," he assured me. "And I'm paying."

"Okay, fine. I'll play."

After witnessing the continual disobedience of my golf ball that day, I decided to spend a lot of money. A new set of clubs, membership dues, and a cohort of fellow addicts fed my near-daily truancy from the responsibilities of my career. The money didn't seem important, but it did add up. I mean, even the dumb, little white glove that you wear on one hand was twenty-five bucks.

That was before God called me to Compassion International. I feel like one of those people who confesses a litany of sins and then discounts it all with, "But that was before I was a Christian."

Now, to the small army of spouses who think golf is evil, I must testify that golf is wonderful. It reveals character, cultivates simplicity, and trains focus. Only those who have mastered the art of accepting their inabilities can walk in the serenity and beauty of a golf course without hurling their golf clubs at nature—the grass, the nearest tree, or into a lake—as my brother once did. Of course, the other option is to drink a lot of beer, careen about the course in a motorized cart, and kick your ball out to a better lie anytime you're unhappy with it. Either way, golf is good.

Maybe you've heard of speed golf. Well, now I play Fast: Golf—I've given up the game (mostly). I have chosen to fast from golf in order to free the time and money for greater purposes. I'm not claiming any nobility, I'm saying that the decision to "not eat" gets practical in a lot of ways. Sometimes it's literal; sometimes it means other things.

Willow Creek Community Church once held a rice-and-beans week in which participants ate nothing but rice and beans for a week. I visited them on the last day of rice-and-beans week, and Bill Hybels warned me, "We're all feeling a little grumpy at this point in the week." Physical hunger is uncomfortable, but it can have a surprising and powerful impact. Going without food is, in a small way, an act of solidarity with the poor—feeling what they feel shapes our spirits. And it can help make poverty personal.

If the strategies for poverty eradication remain abstract and impersonal (policies, foreign investments, agricultural yields, and so on), then they will be detached from the blood supply of collective willpower. But when poverty is personal, when we care enough to become hungry to end it and invest ourselves in that effort, then everything else follows. Isaiah 58 says, "If you pour *yourself* out for the hungry . . ." (v. 10 ESV, emphasis added). It has to be personal.

Mike Foster drives junky cars. He started a club for people

who choose to drive beaters in order to avoid high car payments and insurance costs, and then they use the saved money to support good causes. He called it the Junky Car Club.

Pastor Francis Chan, author of *Crazy Love*, chose to move from a larger house into a smaller one so that he could become more generous toward the things God was calling him to do.

Willow Creek eats Fast: Food. Mike Foster drives Fast: Cars. Francis Chan has Fast: Moves. People working in soup kitchens are living Fast: Time. Companies who support the cause of ending extreme poverty are earning Fast: Profit. What fast will you choose?

Fasting is hard to do alone. It's easier with a group of friends. Gather a group, choose your fast together, and go hungry by choice.

When we die, we will laugh. The life we once knew will seem so small, and our acts of fasting will seem so temporary, we will laugh with joy over those few times we got it right by temporarily giving up something good for the sake of something great.

I chose to fast today as I wrote this chapter. I haven't eaten for nineteen hours, and bacon sounds so good right now. Fasting doesn't require that we give up the good thing permanently. It means giving it up temporarily. It is a temporary abstinence from a good thing for the sake of something great. I may be hungry now, but tomorrow? I'm having bacon!

Life is full of good things. But it's also full of great opportunities. I'm confident that when I die, I won't look back and wish I had played a few more rounds of golf. I'm trying to make sure I don't look back and regret missing those great opportunities. I want to look back and see that I temporarily gave up some good things for the sake of the great things. Call it fast living.

It's time to become good at being hungry.

CHAPTER 26

TEN PERCENT RADICAL

*If I were hungry I would not tell you, for the
world is mine, and all that is in it.*

—GOD (PSALM 50:12)

*If our poor die of hunger, it is not because God
does not care for them. Rather, it is because
neither you nor I are generous enough.*

—MOTHER TERESA, *NO GREATER LOVE*

In May 2009, a secret meeting of billionaires took place in New York. Bill Gates, Warren Buffet, David Rockefeller, Ted Turner, George Soros, and Oprah Winfrey among others were hosted by New York's mayor Michael Bloomberg. They gathered to talk about giving away their money.[1]

According to the 2009 Forbes 400 list, the net worth of the top four hundred American billionaires was $1.2 trillion at the time of the New York gathering. How have they fared through the recession? "The total worth of the Forbes 400 was up 8 percent to

$1.37 trillion, well out-earning the 1 percent rise in the S&P 500 over the same period of time. More than half (217) are richer than they were a year ago."[2]

The New York gathering was just another time when Bill Gates and Warren Buffet again presented a vision and challenge to their peers: "Give away half or more of your wealth." The richest men in America called their peers into a wealth huddle and told them the next play was to give most of it away.

The two are certainly leading by example. Gates established the world's largest charitable foundation by donating thirty-one billion dollars, and Buffet joined him by adding another thirty-one billion in 2006. Both men have pledged to give away over 90 percent of their wealth. They call this commitment "The Giving Pledge."

An impressive number of billionaires are responding to the challenge and joining the pledge. On January 15, 2011, I counted a total of 58 billionaires who have made the pledge (somehow, 58 is a number that shows up a lot for me). You can read each billionaire's explanatory letter of commitment on givingpledge.org. What struck me most about this movement was the language describing their motivation:

> We are inspired by the example set by millions of Americans who give generously (and often at great personal sacrifice) to make the world a better place.[3]

Did you catch that? Fifty-eight billionaires have pledged to give away half or more of their wealth because they're inspired by the "example set by millions of Americans who give generously to make the world a better place." God is at work. The new normal is inspiring waves of good work. The idea of a better world is not a weak, idealistic hope but a gathering storm of intention and action.

Elsewhere Gates describes his motivation more colorfully:

> How many people work on, say, brownie mix? How many
> people work on a soft drink? Is it possible that there should be
> a foundation that has a fifth as many people working on saving
> lives as there are working on Diet Pepsi? I don't know, maybe
> we're too big. Maybe we should be a tenth of what they put into
> improving dog food. . . . Go get 0.1 percent of the scientists
> working on erectile dysfunction to come and work on malaria
> and you will be making a huge contribution.[4]

The leadership shown by Gates and Buffet is truly extraordinary, not only in its generosity but in its motive. Both have
taken hits from cynics accusing them of hidden and self-serving
motives, but such cynical arguments are pretty thin on evidence.
Many of the billionaires, including Gates, have claimed that they
are not religiously motivated. So what's the source of that mysterious, motivating spark in the billionaire's heart?

The billionaire's pledge reminds me of a story from the
Old Testament. Nebuchadnezzar, king of Babylon, laid siege to
Jerusalem, plundered the temple, burned it to the ground, and
hauled off the Jews as slaves for his empire (2 Kings 24). About
fifty years later, the Persian king, Cyrus, destroyed the Babylonian
empire, and according to Ezra 1:1, "The LORD moved the heart of
Cyrus king of Persia" to issue a decree ordering the release of all
captive Jews, ordering non-Jewish community members to provide them with "silver and gold, with goods and livestock, and
with freewill offerings for the temple of God in Jerusalem" (v. 4).

The Jews returned from Babylonian exile with wealth to
rebuild the temple because God moved in the heart of a pagan
king. But God's movement among the pagan kings did not end

with Cyrus. The entire story unfolds across decades of political opposition and violence, but in the end at least three Persian kings—Cyrus, Darius, and Artaxerxes—are moved by God to support the rebuilding of the temple and the restoration of Jerusalem. And it was paid for out of the treasury of a pagan empire. Ezra reacts by praising God, "Praise be to the Lord, the God of our ancestors, who has put it into the king's heart to bring honor to the house of the Lord in Jerusalem in this way" (Ezra 7:27).

I don't expect any billionaires will read this book, but just in case they do, I hope they are not offended by being compared to the kings of Persia. I don't know anything about the faith of today's kings, but they are listed on the Forbes 400, and my faith tells me that God is moving among them for a great purpose. I wouldn't be surprised if some of them are experiencing a joyful bewilderment as a result of their own generosity. The mysterious, inspiring spark of motivation in their souls may remain hidden to them, but I think it's God's work.

To be clear, these pledges are "a moral commitment to give, not a legal contract,"[5] and nearly all the pledged money has yet to be given. The actual giving involves a disbursement of wealth over the span of decades. Skeptics may question whether the billionaires will keep their moral commitments, but I suspect that while a few may fail, many others will discover the truth of Jesus' teaching: "It is more blessed to give than to receive" (Acts 20:35). According to Jesus, giving literally makes you happier than receiving. The billionaires may already be experiencing greater joy and purpose in this call as stewards for a greater cause than the joys they experienced while generating wealth in the first place.

Imagine if all four hundred billionaires on the Forbes list joined the pledge, and let's optimistically suppose that all of them actually followed through on their pledges. About six hundred billion dollars would become available for charitable work. Assuming they are able to transfer that wealth within a span of twenty years (a reasonably optimistic estimate), there would be thirty billion dollars per year available for philanthropy. Staggering! Inspiring! Holy cow!

However, for comparison and perspective, if American Christians (not all of them, just the 138 million who attend church at least twice per month) were to tithe (give 10 percent), it would result in two hundred and fifty billion dollars per year in philanthropy. Over eight times the giving power from the rest of us simply by obeying one of God's biblical principles of generosity.

Smith and Emerson write:

> Ordinary American Christians have within their power the capacity to foster massive and unprecedented spiritual, social, cultural, and economic change that closely reflects their values and interests. In order to achieve such dramatic, world-transforming change, ordinary American Christians simply need to do one thing: start giving reasonably generously from their incomes, let us say 10% of post-tax income.[6]

We have already said that the church is the most resourced, most readied agent to create great social good. The church is unrivaled in its capacity. If we want to respond to the massive challenges of global poverty, then the church is the organization with the legs to get it done.

So how are we stewarding this wealth? On average, Christians keep about 97.1 percent of their money for themselves. Total giving, including church offerings and all tax-deductible contributions to any cause or organization, is 2.9 percent. That might be either discouraging compared to the tithe or encouraging compared to nonreligious Americans who give a measly 0.7 percent. But we need to look more closely at the number because the details hiding within it are important. An excellent and rigorous review of Christian giving is provided in *Passing the Plate* by Christian Smith and Michael Emerson.

Smith and Emerson show that one out of five, or 20 percent, of all American Christians don't give a red cent to anyone for anything. Their zero-giving life drags the average down considerably. But most of those Christians don't attend church either, so one might question the authenticity of their claim to be Christian.[7] If you only look at the 138 million Christians who attend church regularly, the percentage of zero-givers drops to 4.5 percent, and average giving among the church-attending set is 6.2 percent. On the other end of the giving chart, of the 138 million, about 24.8 million of us give 10 percent or more.

In other words, if 20 percent of us aren't giving anything, and another 20 percent are giving 10 percent or more, then we're left with 60 percent (or three out of five) somewhere in the middle. That's the awakening middle, the shifting center, and the power for the new normal. Smith and Emerson conclude that "reasonable generosity"[8] among this middle would generate an *additional* $133.4 billion per year.[9]

For comparison, world-renowned economist Jeff Sachs estimates that ending extreme poverty would require seventy three billion dollars per year over a span of ten years.[10] But that $73 billion is a total cost that could be funded from many sources. Ending poverty is a global responsibility, and the US share would probably be half or less of that $73 billion—around thirty-six billion dollars. Sachs generally treats ending poverty as a government responsibility and sees those dollars in the form of government foreign assistance. If the government paid a third of the cost, corporate philanthropy and the super-rich paid another third, that would leave just twelve billion dollars for the American church to contribute. In other words, the potential for additional giving ($133 billion) by reasonable generosity is tenfold greater than the church's portion of the cost of ending poverty. These admittedly simplistic estimates serve only one point—no matter how you look at it, we have far more than we need to bring an end to extreme poverty. All this assumes that our church's current spending priorities remain unchanged. Yet a change in those priorities might ignite new life in the global church.

Why haven't we already ended extreme poverty? What's holding us back from being more generous? *Passing the Plate* considers nine possible answers to that question, but one that stands out is a significant number of Christians are uninspired by the budget priorities of their churches. Depending on the denomination, between 19 and 47 percent of churchgoers *disagreed* with this statement: "The budget priorities of my congregation are appropriate."[11]

To put it simply, ending extreme poverty is not the object of our generosity. According to the National Congregations Survey data, 57.6 percent of reporting US Christian congregations give no money at all to any social service program. Smith and Emerson conclude, "Most of the money that US Christians currently do give away to congregations ends up getting spent essentially on the givers, primarily for maintaining their own local congregations."[12] This means that salaries, benefits, and supplies account for 75 percent of expenses, 8 percent goes to facilities and improvements, and 11 percent to denominational structures, while 4 percent is donated to other organizations, and 2 percent is offered as direct assistance.

If the church fully awakens to the possibilities of our time, if the legacy of Stephen rises again in this generation, if we fearfully assess the scope of our stewardship and remember our commission to be ambassadors of God's kingdom, then our eyes will again focus on the Author and Perfecter of our faith. His priorities will become our own, and we will endeavor by His Spirit's power to fulfill an unprecedented, history-making testimony of His goodness. The muscles of the good news will flex with a fresh flow of blood as the body of Christ rises to defend the cause of the fatherless, seeks justice for the oppressed, and brings an end to the unjustified and unnecessary suffering of extreme poverty. It's not only our moral obligation and biblical command, it is also our great opportunity as the church to bring glory to the reputation of Jesus Christ and to demonstrate the manifold wisdom of God.

The stakes are high. The risk of failing as stewards is real, and we should learn from the failure of Jesus' treasurer. On the night of his betrayal Jesus spoke to Judas, "'What you are about to do, do quickly.' But no one at the meal understood why Jesus said this to him. Since Judas had charge of the money, some thought Jesus was telling him to buy what was needed for the festival, or to give something to the poor" (John 13:27–29).

The disciples overheard Jesus telling Judas, "What you are about to do, do quickly," but they didn't know what Jesus was talking about. Their assumption that Jesus sent Judas off on a noble errand offers fantastic insight.

The disciples wondered, "What is Jesus spending our money on?" It must be one of two things—to celebrate God's goodness in the Passover Feast, or to demonstrate God's goodness by caring for the poor. The eleven had a different view of money from Judas.

The American church has been entrusted with the purse of the kingdom. Hundreds of millions of fellow disciples live amidst life-threatening poverty,[13] and I wonder if they are assuming we would put the treasuries of the kingdom to one of those two purposes—celebrating God's goodness or demonstrating God's goodness by caring for the poor. One day they will see the books.

Many Christian leaders are shining a fearless light on these realities and calling us to take the radical words of Jesus seriously: "In the same way, those of you who do not give up everything you have cannot be my disciples" (Luke 14:33). Megachurch pastor David Platt, in his inspiring and best-selling book *Radical*, challenges us, "For the sake of 26,000 children who will die today from starvation or preventable disease, I want to risk it all . . . If our lives do not reflect radical compassion for the poor, there is reason to wonder if Christ is really in us at all." He writes further:

> You and I both have a choice.
>> We can stand with the starving or with the overfed.
>> We can identify with poor Lazarus on his way to heaven or with the rich man on his way to hell.
>> We can embrace Jesus while we give away our wealth, or we can walk away from Jesus while we hoard it.[14]

Of course Platt is not the first to call us to generosity for the poor. The legacy of radical Christian compassion and generosity originated with Jesus, reverberated in the stoning of Stephen, shined as the impoverished Macedonian church gave sacrificially out of their poverty to provide cross-national aid to people suffering famine in Jerusalem (2 Cor. 8:2), and the legacy has persevered for two thousand years since. In a more recent example, Platt points to the following quote from John Calvin: "(God) has enjoined upon us frugality and temperance, and has forbidden, that any one should go to excess, taking advantage of his abundance. Let those, then, that have riches . . . consider that their abundance was not intended to be laid out in intemperance or excess, but in relieving the necessities of the brethren."[15] Calvin maintained that half of the church's funds should be allotted specifically for the poor.[16]

I am personally inspired and challenged by Platt and other Christian leaders such as Francis Chan and Shane Claiborne who call us to a radical faith. But, given where we are, perhaps we should stick a practical toe in the radical water. On the journey to a more radical faith, surely a first milestone is to become 10-percent radical in our giving.

We should take a page from the billionaire's playbook by publicly committing to give away 10 percent or more of our wealth.[17] Call it the non-billionaire pledge. Let your light shine, help create the new normal, and put yourself in the vulnerable position by publicly declaring your intention to live on only 90 percent (or less) of what God has given you as income.

Another step to ensure that the treasuries of the kingdom reflect Jesus' priorities would be to share the data in this chapter with your church leaders and humbly ask about your church's budget with regard to the poor.

Bono, when speaking of the philanthropists profiled in *Philanthrocapitalism*, had this to say, "As great as some of the philanthropists are, the real change comes through social movements."[18] But to create a movement, the deepest motives of social change must be ignited. And who among us has the reputation and energy to stir up radical change? Who is willing to do hard things?

CHAPTER 27

THE NEXT GENERATION

*The best time to plant a tree was 20 years
ago. The next best time is now.*

—CHINESE PROVERB

No social change of any significance can occur without the permission of our children. Ending extreme global poverty is a twenty-five-year endeavor. Today's fifteen-year-olds will be turning forty as we run the last (and most difficult) mile, and they will be carrying the baton. How hard they will run then depends on their engagement today. Social change on this scale cannot be achieved by plans or even by organizations alone. It requires an enduring way to live out our faith and the perseverance of a new normal that characterizes the next generation.

We tend to think of children in terms of their needs and vulnerabilities. They need guidance, education, nourishment, and protection from the evil threats of this world. Absolutely true. But we also need to recognize the catalytic power in children for change. They are God's agents and opinion-shapers. This isn't a cliché children-are-the-future argument—of course they're the future. Rather, I want you to recognize the power of young people to change the world.

Twelve-year-old Zach Hunter started a campaign called "Loose Change to Loosen Chains" to raise awareness and money to end modern-day slavery. At age fifteen, he wrote a book called *Be the Change*, and he spoke courageously in hundreds of venues about his passion for justice. Zach's bio begins, "Zach Hunter is 18-years-old and he's leading a new generation of activists who are putting their faith into action to address some of the most serious problems facing the world today."[1]

Zach is not alone. Teen brothers Alex and Brett Harris have a similar passion and have authored a book called *Do Hard Things*. They started a "rebelution" described on the book's jacket as, "A growing movement of young people rebelling against the low expectations of today's culture by choosing to 'do hard things' for the glory of God."[2] The movement holds 1 Timothy 4:12 as its call, "Let no one despise you for your youth, but set the believers an example in speech, in conduct, in love, in faith, in purity" (ESV).

Micah, at age seven, began setting aside money from every allowance, gift, and payment for chores in order to sponsor a child with Compassion along with a matching grant from his grandparents. After three years of saving, he had enough to sponsor for the first year and began supporting a child in Uganda, a commitment he has kept for six years and counting. Similarly, Stephanie was sixteen when she worked two jobs cleaning hotel rooms in order to earn enough money to sponsor two children with Compassion. The ranks of this emerging generation are filled with young men and women of character, vision, resolve, and action.

God's work through young people to change society is not a new strategy. God has been working through young people for thousands of years. He spoke to a little boy named Samuel in order to correct the evil of religious leaders who were "fattening themselves" with offerings meant for the Lord (1 Sam. 2–3). Josiah became the king of Israel when he was only eight years old, eventually purging Israel of idols and leading a spiritual revival (2 Chron. 34). God Himself entered the world by impregnating and being birthed by a teenage girl. The Bible is filled with examples of children and youth who are agents of God's work.

When I see the inspiring examples of young people today, their engagement with the world and determination to make it a better place give me hope. I compare today's Christian youth with my own experience as a young person and trust God that the world will be better off in their hands. If I had saved money at age seven, I wouldn't have lasted a month. I probably would have dumped the money jar to buy a Star Wars X-wing fighter.

I didn't grow up in a Christian home, but when I was in seventh grade my parents decided to fix the family by taking us to church. I was mildly curious about church since it seemed like a lot of other kids went. And that's when I first discovered youth group.

On my first night at youth group, I went downstairs and found a few members of the youth group huddled around a card table. They were snickering and glancing over their shoulders trying to subdue the inner thrill of a secret. I cautiously approached the huddle and discovered the source of the thrill. Someone had played a four-letter word in the Scrabble game. Unsure how to respond, I walked on to see what else was happening.

I think I expected youth group would have something to do with religious instruction. I thought they would talk about the

Bible or virtue or something. Whatever I expected to find, I'm sure I didn't expect Chubby Bunny.

I was an uninitiated, non-Christian, and Chubby Bunny created a disturbing and bewildering uncertainty for me. I'd never seen anything like it—puberty-infected youth jammed increasing numbers of marshmallows into their mouths, the shrill voices of their peers throttling the competitors in a wild-eyed frenzy to see which kid could shove the most marshmallows in and still articulate "Chubby Bunny." The contest crescendoed with enormous blobs of half-dissolved marshmallow oozing out of thinly stretched lips and falling off the chins of the losers while the victor pushed a deeply muffled "chhbb bnnn" through a wad of eighteen marshmallows moments before he gagged and nearly vomited in the host's basement. So, that's what we were up to as twelve-year-olds—the age at which Zach Hunter started a campaign to end modern-day slavery.

Although I have optimism for today's youth, they face serious threats. We have an adversary who recognizes the strategic importance of young people, and we are in a fight for their minds and hearts. Just as God often works through young people, our adversary is tireless in his efforts to deceive, indoctrinate, and distract them. John the Baptist was beheaded at a girl's request. And there are plenty of modern examples that illustrate the dark possibilities of youth being seduced into enlisting with the adversary.

The Nazi party established the Hitler Youth in 1922. Within a year it had one thousand members, within three years, five thousand, and by 1932 the number had climbed to 107,000 members. Its energy carried the Nazis to power in Germany. The following year, the Hitler Youth numbered 2.3 million, and the world was already on its way to inevitable war, thanks in large part to the ideologies that germinated in those young German minds. Zero to war in ten years.

Corporate America also recognizes the strategic importance of children and youth, spending billions on youth marketing strategies to achieve brand recognition and new markets among the young. Our children watch over twenty thousand thirty-second television ads every year. Young American Christians ages eight to eighteen consume an average of seven hours and thirty-eight minutes of visual media per day.[3] But that figure doesn't count multitasking media, because if you add engaging multiple media sources at the same time the figure jumps to ten hours and forty-five minutes per day.

Most of those channels exist to serve an industry with the singular goal of selling stuff by creating discontent in the mind of the child consumer. Our children are in front of advertisements for more hours every day than they spend at school or engaged in all other conscious activity combined. This is the altar of the god whose bible is written on Madison Avenue.

Consequently our children witness over eight thousand murders by the time they reach the fifth grade. Even our children's dreams have changed. In the 1960s, children told us their greatest ambitions were to be doctors, and today their greatest dreams are to be rich. But the media isn't entirely to blame. I wonder what we ourselves could do to inspire bigger dreams and higher expectations in our kids. "If anything is excellent or praiseworthy—think about such things" (Phil. 4:8).

When my kids were younger, they went to "Adventure Quest" at our church. It isn't called Sunday school anymore. The rooms were themed as London, Venice, or some other global city, and Indiana Jones music played in the background.

One day I went to get one of my boys, which required turning in a bar-coded card that was bleeped into the system to verify I wasn't abducting someone else's kid. I asked him about class, and he told me they had made Resurrection Rolls. He explained that Jesus was represented by a marshmallow wrapped in a pastry—the Shroud of Turin-Pillsbury, I guess—and then you eat him.

I nodded and "uh-huhed" as he explained, but I couldn't get my head around the concept. Jesus, the marshmallow you eat. Probably Chubby-Bunny style.

I know Chubby Bunny and Resurrection Rolls are well-intended efforts to overcome the dreaded reputation of church being boring. But it feels like we're trying to compete with our entertainment-consumer culture, and I'm not sure it's working.

If we intend to raise up an army of Christ-followers who will pursue justice for the oppressed and who will fight the adversary in a world afflicted by poverty, then we must begin training our youth for that fight. They are our greatest assets. They are young and full of energy. They are uncompromising idealists, and they actually believe that God is all-powerful. To end extreme poverty for good requires nurturing the strength and future of the church—our youth. They want to change the world. They are sick of all the weak substitutes, placebos of fun, and some of them are Zach Hunters who need to be taken seriously. We should listen to them, challenge them, live our own lives in ways that demonstrate world-changing intentions, and save the marshmallows for a camping trip or a mug of hot chocolate.

CHAPTER 28

THORNS AND PROMISES

Command those who are rich in this present world not
to be arrogant nor to put their hope in wealth, which is so
uncertain, but to put their hope in God, who richly provides
us with everything for our enjoyment. Command them
to do good, to be rich in good deeds, and to be generous
and willing to share. In this way they will lay up treasure
for themselves as a firm foundation for the coming age,
so that they may take hold of the life that is truly life.

—1 TIMOTHY 6:17–19

You wicked, lazy servant! Throw that worthless servant outside, into the darkness, where there will be weeping and gnashing of teeth" (Matt. 25:26, 30). Incredibly, Jesus said these words. What made Him use such strong language?

Our motivation to work for the end of extreme poverty should be rooted in our love for God and our love for the poor. It may be strengthened when we realize our efforts aren't futile—instead they are likely to succeed. Yet there is another motivation and, to be honest, I've been reluctant to write about it. It is a fearful theme in Scripture.

In Luke 16, Jesus tells the story of a manager responsible for his master's affairs, but who has been wasting his master's resources. The master is on the brink of firing him when the manager executes a series of shrewdly generous acts that earn the commendation of his master.

Jesus concludes, "So if you have not been trustworthy in handling worldly wealth, who will trust you with true riches?" (v. 11). What are the "true riches" that you won't receive if you fail to manage your money well?

Then Jesus drives the point home, "'You cannot serve both God and money.' The Pharisees, who loved money, heard all this and were sneering at Jesus" (vv. 13–14).

Jesus' lesson on stewardship sets the stage for the next story in Luke 16—the story of the rich man and Lazarus. Jesus begins:

There was a rich man who was dressed in purple and fine linen and lived in luxury every day. At his gate was laid a beggar named Lazarus, covered with sores and longing to eat what fell from the rich man's table. Even the dogs came and licked his sores.

The time came when the beggar died and the angels carried him to Abraham's side. The rich man also died and was buried. In Hades, where he was in torment, he looked up and saw Abraham far away, with Lazarus by his side. So he called to him, "Father Abraham, have pity on me and send Lazarus to dip the tip of his finger in water and cool my tongue, because I am in agony in this fire."

But Abraham replied, "Son, remember that in your lifetime you received your good things, while Lazarus received bad things, but now he is comforted here and you are in agony." (vv. 19–25)

In the rich man's final plea, he says, "'Then I beg you, father, send Lazarus to my family, for I have five brothers. Let him warn them, so that they will not also come to this place of torment'" (vv. 27–28).

Warn them of what? What if you had five minutes with the rich man? What would he say to you?

This is not the only time Jesus ties together wealth, poverty, and eternal judgment.

In Matthew 25, Jesus again teaches about money management and accountability. He tells the story of three men (servants) who are entrusted with different amounts of money. Two of them invest it and yield a return, but one is fearful and hides the money in the ground. When the master calls them to account for their use of the funds, he has harsh words for the servant who did not invest: "You wicked, lazy servant!" (v. 26). And, "Throw that worthless servant outside, into the darkness, where there will be weeping and gnashing of teeth" (v. 30).

The simple point is that if we stewards aren't making good investments with what we've been given, we are squandering it, and that carries harsh consequences.

After telling this story, Jesus goes on to describe Judgment Day itself. He speaks of a process of separation in which people are sorted to the left and to the right in front of the King's throne. To those on the right the King says, "Come, you who are blessed by my Father; take your inheritance, the kingdom prepared for you since the creation of the world. For I was hungry and you gave me something to eat, I was thirsty and you gave me something to drink, I was a stranger and you invited me in, I needed clothes and you clothed me, I was sick and you looked after me, I was in prison and you came to visit me" (vv. 34–36).

To those on the left the King says, "Depart from me, you who are cursed, into the eternal fire prepared for the devil and his angels. For I was hungry and you gave me nothing to eat, I was thirsty and you gave me nothing to drink, I was a stranger and you did not invite me in, I needed clothes and you did not clothe me, I was sick and in prison and you did not look after me" (vv. 41–43).

Jesus then personally identifies with the poor—the hungry, the thirsty, the unknown people, the ones without clothing, the sick and imprisoned. He says that what was done for these people was actually done for Him. The difference in how the two groups of people treated the poor determined how they were judged, and the judgment was severe.

Similar teaching is found in Matthew 13, where Jesus tells a parable about a farmer sowing seed. The seed represents the message about the kingdom, and some of that seed falls among the thorns. Jesus explains, "The seed falling among the thorns refers to someone who hears the word, but the worries of this life and the deceitfulness of wealth choke the word, making it unfruitful" (v. 22).

We live among the thorns, and the danger of their choking power is real. Jesus often associated "unfruitfulness" with eternal consequences. In perhaps the most shocking statement about the choking power of wealth, Jesus says, "It is easier for a camel to go through the eye of a needle than for someone who is rich to enter the kingdom of God" (Matt. 19:24).

Sometimes I read Scripture with fear—I think it's unwise to read these words too easily. As we consider our multimillion-dollar church buildings, media systems, and the debt with which they are financed, we must ask whom they are designed to serve.

We have preoccupied the passions of the bride of Christ in America by transfusing her holy blood with our culture's blood of amusement and consumerism. She has been weakened by our syncretism. The power and resources already entrusted to us by God were sufficient to end extreme poverty, but we haven't always invested wisely. It's not too late to be a shrewd manager. Not too late to stop and care for Lazarus. Not too late to dig the talent back up out of the ground and put it to good use. Not too late for generous action.

Jesus' teaching on the relationship between money (often the idolizing love of it), the treatment of the poor, and God's judgment is similar to God's word through the prophets. For example, the sins of Sodom so angered God that He destroyed the city and its people. Most Christians think of the sins of Sodom as sexual deviance, yet consider the words of Ezekiel 16: "Now this was the sin of your sister Sodom: She and her daughters were arrogant, overfed and unconcerned; they did not help the poor and needy" (v. 49).

Arrogant, overfed, and unconcerned. I cannot imagine a more brutal indictment.

Jeremiah also addresses the themes of money management, the poor, and status of relationship with God. He writes of a leader who pursued a lifestyle of material wealth and compares him to his father who did what was right. Jeremiah describes the father, "'He defended the cause of the poor and needy, and so all went well. Is that not what it means to know me?' declares the LORD" (Jer. 22:16).

Read that again—it's too important to miss.

Scripture is flooded with these messages: calling us to remember the poor (Gal. 2:10), reminding us that "religion that our father accepts as pure and faultless" requires the care of orphans and widows (James 1:27), warning us that doing nothing about hungry people is evidence of a dead faith (James 2:15–17), questioning how the love of God can be in us if we have material possessions and don't respond to people in need (1 John 3:17), and many more.

Among all these scriptures, Isaiah 58 is a powerful embodiment of the theme. In Isaiah 57:17, God describes His rage at man's "sinful greed," but also commits to healing him. And so Isaiah 58 opens with a declaration against the sin of religious shows that are offered as a substitute for the True Fast God desires. As we discussed earlier, Isaiah warns the people that they are in the presence of an unlistening God. But he also shows them how to regain His ear by urging the people to live the True Fast.

The way forward is not simply an escape hatch from a future in hell, as you might be tempted to think by reading Jesus' stories. It's not just a way for the shrewd manager to avoid getting fired or for the lazy servant to avoid being thrown outside. The way forward is *toward* a destination.

The stern warning is given, but not without its joyful counterpart—the incredible promise.

The steward who invested wisely is invited to, "Come and share your master's happiness!" (Matt. 25:21).

Those who cared for the poor are told, "Come, you who are blessed by my Father; take your inheritance, the kingdom prepared for you since the creation of the world" (v. 34).

So, too, in Isaiah 58 the destination of promise is offered.

If you respond to the grievous, sacred moment of our generation by breaking the chains of injustice (v. 6), sharing your food with the hungry, providing for the poor wanderer (v. 7), pouring yourself out for the hungry, and satisfying the needs of the oppressed (v. 10), then:

Your light will break forth like the dawn,
and your healing will quickly appear;
then your righteousness will go before you,
and the glory of the LORD will be your rear guard.
Then you will call; and the LORD will answer . . .
He will satisfy your needs in a sun-scorched land and will
     strengthen your frame.
You will be like a well-watered garden, like a spring whose
     waters never fail . . .
You will be called "Repairer of Broken Walls" and "Restorer of
     Streets with Dwellings . . ."
Then you will find your joy in the LORD. (Is. 58:8–9, 11, 12,
     14)

The scriptures tell us of an early community of believers who lived in such a way that they eradicated poverty from their midst (Acts 4:34). Thousands were added to their numbers daily. They flourished, witnessed the miracles of God, and radically transformed the known world. God is ready to do it again, if we are willing to join Him.

CHAPTER 29

THE HISTORY WE HOPE TO WRITE

Look at the nations and watch—and be utterly
amazed. For I am going to do something in your days
that you would not believe, even if you were told.

—HABAKKUK 1:5

n 2035, headlines declared the end of pandemic poverty. For the first time in human history, over 98 percent of humanity lived in a state of economic sufficiency. Famine and hunger were permanently abolished. Children born in Africa were as likely to have a fifth birthday party as children born in America. School completion and literacy rates climbed above 90 percent. Death by mosquito was eradicated. The invisible terrorists in African drinking water were disarmed, eliminated, or rendered harmless.

Early in the twenty-first century an awakening stirred the Christian movement. Church leaders summoned boldness to move in new directions. Their awakening greatly advanced the kingdom and the good of the world which God so loved.

The twenty-first-century Christians embraced the entirety of their gospel—the truths it proclaims and the muscles it demands—with a new integrity. They did not deteriorate into humanist liberalism, as some had feared. Nor did they pile works on top of God's grace in a vain effort to earn God's pardon. They simply sought to be like Jesus because they loved Him.

Local communities of faith, aligned by a common dependency and quest for God's guidance, worked together as the transformative agents, salt and light, that created the better world. These local communities of faith strongly resembled the earliest Christian communities. Yet unlike any time in their history, these twenty-first-century ecclesia were globally connected and globally influential. They worked together for a better world without a strident triumphalism that fueled pride, but with the humble faithfulness that characterized them in their finest moments of history.

Christians found many opportunities to make the world better, but one Goliath became a major focus—extreme poverty. The Christian response to the suffering of the poor shifted from an anemic and guilt-laden duty to a hope-filled opportunity. The twenty-first-century Christians formed a new expectation of their futures. They determined that their world truly did not need to have children dying of preventable causes such as dirty water. They decided it wasn't normal after all. The pivotal moment that unleashed all this new energy came when Christians broke from the tyranny of their own low expectations.

For these Christians, ending poverty was not a cause or an issue. It was personal. It was about people, motivated by the ones they knew and loved. People they had prayed with and stood shoulder to shoulder with in worship. It was about love for people they had called brothers and sisters. People whose faith had inspired and humbled them. And it was about serving Jesus.

The twenty-first-century Christians embraced their legacy—recognizing who they really were and the power dwelling within them. The examples of Christians across the two thousand years of their movement inspired new courage and deeper self-sacrifice. They were shocked by the rapid progress against poverty and drew together to mount a final impassioned and unified effort to banish it altogether.

These Christians recognized the grievous, sacred moment of their generation. Not eating was their natural response to the grievous realities of extreme poverty as well as the sacred realities of their generation's unprecedented opportunity. With high expectations they became profoundly and wonderfully hungry, and that hunger formed an unstoppable engine of social change.

Christians created a new culture of effective generosity and reoriented the culture of consumerism. The groundswell of new hunger shaped markets for social good, shifted the winds of political influence, and recalibrated the budgets of the church. They focused their resources on effective work as best they knew how.

The 138 million church-attending American Christians looked at the 2.5 trillion dollars God had given them in annual income and realized that God had loaned them the power to do incredible things. They ached when they realized they were spending 97.1 percent of their incomes on themselves. Their church leaders repented for having spent 96 percent of the offerings on buildings, carpets, and staff hired for the benefit of the givers. They launched a new movement of effective Christian generosity, and brave intelligence compelled them to work across sectors with government and with business.

They leveraged globalization for good. They employed amazing new communication technologies. They translated the rapid increases in international travel into grassroots solidarity between northern and southern hemispheres. They built structures to support this new, global solidarity. They celebrated a rise in southern-hemisphere Christian leadership. It all fueled a collision of ideas, intentions, and actions.

Christians also created a powerful voice of influence on behalf of the poor and insisted that their governments fix and fund their foreign-assistance programs. The governments of donor nations purged the quagmire and bureaucracy of foreign aid, becoming serious about enabling protection and opportunity for the vulnerable. They stopped using aid as a tool of geo-political self-interest. Many governments kept the promises they expressed in the Millennium Development Goals.

The collective effort in food security, health, and education increased the creative and productive capacities of impoverished nations. New leadership rooted out corruption and strengthened the integrity of governments to lead on behalf of their people. These changes attracted business investments and employment opportunities even as Christians created market demand for goods produced in impoverished countries. Hundreds of millions of people escaped extreme poverty, bringing the global pandemic of extreme poverty to an end.

An ancient idea fueled this world-changing Christian work. A spiritual discipline that Jesus Himself practiced. Choosing hunger. Foregoing something good in exchange for a greater good. The True Fast of Isaiah 58 redefined Christian action.

In 2035, the worldwide extreme poverty rate fell below 2 percent—a threshold that was widely agreed to signify the end of the global pandemic of poverty. Over 98 percent of humanity had the opportunity and capacity to earn enough income to meet their most basic needs. Those who still had needs were cared for through the systems of benevolence in their own societies. The instruments of foreign assistance became obsolete.

Because of this work and its results, the nations gained a new admiration for the Christian movement. The name of Jesus was held in high regard. His people gave Him the glory.

After the twenty-first-century Christians died, what they did continued to be celebrated. The children of the twenty-second century learned about the work to end poverty like the children of the twentieth century had learned about the end of the slave trade. And they were inspired to keep that legacy as they continued God's work of reconciliation, facing off against the persisting evils of humanity. They never placed their hopes in an earthly utopia, but in Christ and His cause.

CHAPTER 30

RAISING HOPE

"Son of man, can these bones live?"

—EZEKIEL 37:3

Hope starts in the guts. People think hope is fluffy, but it's not. Because it takes courage to believe there's a way out when things are grim. Hope is that salty determination that gets a fighter back up off the mat. It's that stubborn grit that says, "This is not the end." It's what you cling to when the whole world starts swirling after you receive that diagnosis. It might be the toughest substance around. You just need a little of it to carry you forward through hard places. But you do need a little of it.

As tough as hope is, it's not invincible. The chill of expired hope is a dreadful human condition. You've probably seen it. Hope-expired lives are like a graveyard with tombstones etched with the names of broken marriages, abandoned ideas, and suicides. Tragically, for millions of the world's poor, the flame of hope has died. Extinguished by one too many blows from the hardship of poverty. Re-igniting that flame is incredibly difficult, yet without that flame no way through, no way out, will help. Without hope, opportunities will be left untested, and fate will settle like dust across the future.

I don't know what your challenges look like, but I can guarantee you that overcoming them will require three things: a strong vision of the problem-solved future, a bold idea about how to get there, and enough hope in your guts to give it a try. It's no different for the poor. Only that their problems are bigger, their ideas must be bolder, and they have few reasons to hope. Their lives are a seemingly endless sea of insurmountable obstacles. Hope needs a reason.

Hope must have options. It's not enough to believe in a better future. There must be a way to get there. Without a fighting chance, hope can twist into its dark twin—wishful thinking. Wishful thinking dreams all day and does nobody any good. If there is a fear in me as I write, it is that a reader might read, soak in all the possibilities for themselves and for the poor and for the church, and yet finish reading not with hope but with wishful thinking. May God fill our hearts with solid hope instead. The kind of hope that moves out, changes lives, and grows a testimony.

What proof do we have that hope, and not wishful thinking, has been established in our hearts? The proof of hope is action. My assumption from the start has been that you are already engaged in the cause. Your heart is increasingly aligned with God's, and you are living as a steward of resources and influence for the advance of compassion and justice. For that, for your heart and sacrifice, I praise God and pray that you are encouraged and affirmed in your work. Yet there may still be an important question—what works? Many of us are deeply committed to effective stewardship and good development. We want to be sure that our helping does not hurt.

Of all the anti-poverty work that I have seen around the world—and there are many tremendous efforts to join and support—there is one simple and practical path that I chose to follow personally over twenty years ago. After two decades it remains, in my opinion, unrivaled in simplicity and impact. It is a profound strategy that is easily underestimated. I chose to sponsor a child with Compassion. I am specific about the organization because not all sponsorship agencies are the same; in fact they are quite different. I won't elaborate on those differences, but I will point to the essence of Compassion's Christ-centered program that is vital to its proven success—hope.

The wonderful truth is that a child is born with his or her candle of hope already burning. That little candle is incredibly resilient. She has not yet faced the sea of insurmountable obstacles. He has not yet heard the whispering, insidious lie of poverty—"you don't matter." In that little child is all the potential to overcome poverty in her own life and then to lift others around her. And her hope is still alight. While it is extremely difficult to relight that flame in a hope-expired heart (often in adults), it is far easier to shelter that flame and sustain it in a child. In a way, you can raise hope when you sponsor a child.

In Compassion's programs children develop what they call, "My Plan for Tomorrow." It allows kids to express a vision for their futures. It is a canvas upon which they paint their hopes. For you and I, to ask our kids the question, "What do you want to be when you grow up?" may seem like an easy and familiar question and we can readily imagine our kids answering—"fireman, nurse, teacher, football player, or pilot." But for the child in extreme poverty it is sadly common to ask that question only to face a blank stare as if the question itself was incomprehensible. Many adult examples of such careers simply do not exist in their world, and those that do can seem utterly beyond the grasp of a kid who's just hoping for a meal tonight. "My Plan for Tomorrow" is not just a tool in the Compassion program; it's a mindset of possibilities.

As a Compassion sponsor you can participate in shaping a child's sense of possibility by writing him or her encouraging letters, expressing hopes for her future, and reminding her that God loves her and has a plan for her life. Ask a kid in Compassion's program what they want to be when they grow up and it's not uncommon to hear, "teacher" or "pilot" (as Jacki told me), and every now and then you'll come across a future president. Of course the difference between hope and wishful thinking is having a way forward and taking the action needed to move down that path.

If these little hopers are going to have a fighting chance at becoming teachers, nurses, business-owners, or even possibly a president then they will need more than just encouragement. They will need to grow strong in mind and body and in healthy relationships with others. They need protection from harm and opportunity to grow into the young men and women God intended them to be. To achieve that goal, children in Compassion's church-partnered program are provided support to ensure education, health, nutrition, and other basic needs. These provide the ways forward to that hoped-for future. And children are taught about the love of God—the reason for hope. These things, along with positive role models and a canopy of loving adults, allow children in poverty to thrive. It gives them a chance, not a guarantee, to overcome poverty. Many do.

Development is about people. People are the problem, and people are the solution. It is about who we are, who they are, and how we see ourselves in relationship. The programs that work are the ones that develop people. Programs that grow the capacities of people, that protect people from threat, that increase the range of their choices, and that give them opportunities to thrive are the programs that work. The season of "people development" with the greatest potential impact is childhood and the most successful child development strategies are comprehensive (holistic) and long-term.

When we think about the causes of extreme poverty we can point to structures, economies, business practices, legal and justice concerns, but all those things are about people. People build the structures, grow the economies, launch the businesses, establish and enforce the laws. What kind of people do we need to build?

Healthy, educated, responsible, skilled . . . many things are needed. But above all we must raise hope. And that leads to a final question for you and me. What kind of people do *we* need to be?

If we are to build hope in others it will require something of us. To give it you must have it. Such hope flows out of your faith in God. That hope shapes how you see yourself, your future, and also how your life can be used by God to raise hope in others. But the proof that it is hope and not wishful thinking is found in your action. Action follows decisions. So, in the end, it's your call.

In all my prayers for all of you, I always pray with joy because of your partnership in the gospel from the first day until now, being confident of this, that he who began a good work in you will carry it on to completion until the day of Christ Jesus.

—PHILIPPIANS 1:4-6

ENDNOTES

CHAPTER 5

1. Tony Carnes, "Can We Defeat Poverty?" *Christianity Today,* October 2005, http://www.christianitytoday.com/ct/2005/october/19.38.html.
2. During 2000–2008, global mortality attributed to measles declined by 78 percent, from an estimated 733,000 deaths in 2000 to 164,000 in 2008. Centers for Disease Control, "Global Measles Mortality 2000—2008," *Morbidity and Mortality Weekly Report,* December 4, 2009, vol. 58, no. 47: 1321–1326, http://www.cdc.gov/mmwr/preview/mmwrhtml/mm6202a3.htm.
3. World Health Organization, *World Malaria Report 2013* (Geneva, Switzerland: WHO Press, 2008), http://www.who.int/malaria/publications/world_malaria_report_2013/report/en/index.html.
4. UNICEF, *Childinfo: Monitoring the Situation of Children and Women,* November 2009, http://www.who.int/gho/child_health/mortality_under_five_text/en.
5. United Nations, *The Millennium Development Goals Report 2010* (New York: United Nations, 2010), http://www.un.org/millenniumgoals/pdf/report-2013/mdg-report-2013-english.pdf, (page 14).
6. UNAIDS, *UNAIDS Report on the Global AIDS Epidemic,* 2012, http://www.unaids.org/en/media/unaids/contentassets/documents/epidemiology/2012/gr2012/20121120_UNAIDS_Global_Report_2012_en.pdf.
7. Data from consolidated sources. For comprehensive and country-specific data, visit http://www.gapminder.org.

8. Francois Bourguignon and Christian Morrisson, "Inequality Among World Citizens: 1820–1992," *American Economic Review*, September 2002, vol. 92, no.4: 727–744, http://www.aeaweb.org/articles.php?doi=10.1257/00028280260344443&fnd=s.
9. http://povertydata.worldbank.org/poverty/home.
10. http://www.worldbank.org/en/news/press-release/2013/10/01/world-bank-group-bold-steps-accept-smart-risks-help-end-poverty-jim-yong-kim
11. http://www.brookings.edu/research/reports/2013/04/ending-extreme-poverty-chandy

CHAPTER 6

1. John Ortberg, "God Give Me Another Mountain," *Outcomes Magazine*, Spring 2010, 18.
2. Gabe Lyons, *The Next Christians* (New York: Doubleday Religion, 2010), 202.
3. Max Lucado, *Outlive Your Life* (Nashville: Thomas Nelson, 2010), 92.

CHAPTER 7

1. Rick Warren, *The Purpose Driven Life* (Grand Rapids: Zondervan, 2002).
2. H. G. Wells, *The Outline of History* (New York: Macmillan, 1921), 418.
3. Dallas Willard, *The Divine Conspiracy* (New York: HarperOne, 1998), 28.
4. David Platt, *Radical* (Colorado Springs: Multnomah, 2010), 109.

CHAPTER 8

1. Scot McKnight, *Fasting* (Nashville: Thomas Nelson, 2010), xx.
2. Ibid., xxii.
3. Ibid., 123.
4. Peter Singer, *The Life You Can Save* (New York: Random House, 2009), 34.
5. Christian Smith, Michael O. Emerson, and Patricia Snell, *Passing the Plate* (New York: Oxford University Press, 2008), 54.

CHAPTER 9

1. According to UNICEF's 2010 annual report, 1.1 billion people still practice open defecation simply because they have no other option. UNICEF, "Progress for Children: Achieving the MGDs with Equity," *UNICEF Annual Report*, September 2010, no. 9, http://www.unicef.org/publications/files/Progress_for_ Children-No.9_EN_081710.pdf.

2. UNICEF's 2010 annual report. In 1990, 77 percent of the world had access to clean water, but in 2008, 87 percent had access. Ibid.

3. This estimate is a middle figure derived from various estimates from the World Bank, WHO, UNICEF, and UNDP. The World Bank Policy Research Working Paper, "Development Goals: History, Prospects and Costs," by Shantayanan Devarajan, Margaret J. Miller, and Eric V. Swanson estimates the cost of reaching "basic levels of coverage . . . in water and sanitation" to be nine billion dollars at the low end, and thirty billion dollars a year for "achieving universal coverage" for water and sanitation. The same report concludes that, "taking these estimates and their caveats together, we estimate that the cost . . . is between $5 and $21 billion." The United Nations Development Programme estimates that "universal access (to water and sanitation) would (cost) $20–$30 billion" and that not addressing the problem will "cost roughly nine times more than resolving it." Another United Nations document states, "Providing safe drinking water and sanitation to those lacking them requires massive investment— estimated at $14–$30 billion per year in addition to current annual spending levels."

4. World Health Organization, "Global measles deaths drop by 78%, but resurgence likely," World Health Organization Joint News Release with American Red Cross, CDC, UN Foundation, UNICEF, and WHO, December 3, 2009, http://www.who.int/ mediacentre/news/releases/2009/measles_mdg_20091203/en/.

5. World Health Organization, *World Health Statistics 2010 Report*, (Geneva, Switzerland: WHO Press, 2010), http://www.who.int/ gho/publications/world_health_statistics/EN_WHS10_Full.pdf.

CHAPTER 10

1. North Ridge earthquake was 6.9, and Haiti was 7.0.
2. David van Biema and Dan Kray, "Faith or Healing? Why the Law Can't Do a Thing About the Infant-Mortality Rate of an Oregon Sect," *TIME Magazine*, August 31, 1998, vol. 152, no. 9; "Faith Healing," *PBS Religion and Ethics Newsweekly*, April 16, 1999, no. 233; Nicole Dungca, "Jeffrey and Marci Beagley Sentenced to 16 Months of Prison for Their Son's Faith-healing Death," *The Oregonian*, March 8, 2010.
3. "Overall, the lives of an estimated 2.5 million children under 5 years old are saved each year as a result of immunization for vaccine-preventable diseases. Immunization has greatly reduced the number of measles deaths from an estimated 733,000 in 2000 to 164,000 in 2008." (UNICEF 2010 annual report) UNICEF, "Progress for Children: Achieving the MGDs with Equity," *UNICEF Annual Report*, September 2010, no. 9, http://www .unicef.org/publications/files/Progress_for_Children-No.9_ EN_081710.pdf.
4. The under-five mortality rate is 8 per 1000 live births in the US (similar in other developed countries) compared to two hundred (20 percent) in countries that do not have basic medical services such as antibiotics or vaccines. Thankfully nearly all countries are now benefitting from these technologies, and rates of childhood death are dropping even in the toughest countries.
5. Roger Thurow and Scott Kilman, *Enough* (Cambridge, MA: Public Affairs, 2010), x.
6. Ibid., xi.

CHAPTER 11

1. Bryant Myers, *Walking with the Poor: Principles and Practices of Transformational Development* (Maryknoll, NY: Orbis Books, 2011).

CHAPTER 12

1. "(This Mary, whose brother Lazarus now lay sick, was the same

one who poured perfume on the Lord and wiped his feet with her hair.)" (John 11:2).

2. Jesus was referring to extreme economic poverty in this verse. The word *poor* in Scripture means those with unmet basic human needs (hungry, sick, unsheltered, naked). It does not refer to relative poverty or to poverty as a metaphor for our spiritual or social conditions. The entire conflict with Judas centered on the financial value of the perfume and the giving of money to help the poor. Judas certainly wasn't arguing that the money should have been given to the "spiritually poor" Pharisees!

3. Some Bibles cross-reference Jesus' statement to Deuteronomy 15:11. Jesus certainly knew and quoted from Moses (specifically Deuteronomy) but in each case when He does so, there is a near-perfect match between the Greek in the gospel account and the Greek version of the Old Testament passage in reference (Septuagint). In this case, however, there is no match at all, so it should not be considered as a quote. Whether Jesus was inferring a reference to Deuteronomy could be debated, but in the heat of the moment—defending a trembling woman at His feet from the attack of a greedy treasurer—it seems unlikely. A rationale for such inference has been offered by others but seems unnecessarily complex.

CHAPTER 13

1. Anti-poverty work is often called "development."

2. Bryant Myers uses the term "god-complexes" to refer to the arrogant tendency of the non-poor to see themselves as saviors with solutions for the poor and therefore a right to act upon the poor with impunity. He also calls this "playing God in the lives of the poor." Bryant Myers, *Walking with the Poor: Principles and Practices of Transformational Development,* (Maryknoll, NY: Orbis Books, 2011).

3. I'm not referring to "relative poverty" (those whose incomes are low relative to their society's average income) or to poverty as a metaphor.

4. The $1.25 is the World Bank standard absolute poverty line adjusted for purchasing power parity to the 2005 US dollar. In other

words, it is equivalent to an American trying to live on $1.25 per day.
5. The "end of extreme global poverty" does not mean a world in which no single individual lives on less than $1.25 per day. There will always be sporadic cases of self-induced destitution. Rather, the end of extreme global poverty is the end of a condition plaguing massive segments of humanity. It will no longer be pandemic. There may still be some pockets, but they will be the exception—more like outbreaks. To be precise, the "end of extreme global poverty" means a global extreme poverty rate below 2 percent. From that point we will need to work on the "basic poverty" rate (people living below $2 per day) as we move toward global sufficiency.

CHAPTER 15

1. Norman Grubb and C. T. Studd, *Cricketer and Pioneer* (Fort Washington, PA: CLC Publications, 2001), 120–21.

CHAPTER 17

1. Philip Schaff, et al., *Nicene and Post-Nicene Fathers: Series II*, Vol. I and VII, 1885.
2. James Hunter, *To Change the World* (New York: Oxford University Press, 2010).
3. Emperor Julian, Epistle to the Pagan High Priests. Also referenced by Hunter in *To Change the World*.
4. Rodney Stark, *The Rise of Christianity: A Sociologist Reconsiders History* (Princeton, NJ: Princeton University Press, 1996), 155.

CHAPTER 19

1. I refer to "the media" as the collective tools of communication through which commercial interests are promoted. (I realize this is not a technically accurate use of the term, but it's good enough.) Media are instruments of social influence offering reflections or projections of culture, which we find entertaining. It uses that entertainment value to create a state of "strategic discontent" within us. "Strategic discontent" is the goal of "advertising." That discontent incites our consumerism, distracts our affections, and leaves us in debt.

2. Walter Rauschenbusch, *Christianity and the Social Crisis* (New York: The Macmillan Company, 1913).
3. Mother Teresa, *No Greater Love* (New York: Mjf Books, 2000).

CHAPTER 20
1. C.S. Lewis, *The Screwtape Letters* (New York: HarperCollins Publishers, 2001).

CHAPTER 21
1. Thomas Merton, *No Man Is an Island* (New York: Fall River Press, 2003), 16.
2. For clarity, I will refer to the global body of Christ-followers who permeate all aspects of society as the Church with a capital "C," and local Christian congregations as churches with a lowercase "c." The churches and parachurch organizations roughly describe the Christian component of the social sector.

CHAPTER 22
1. George W. Bush, "America's Global Fight Against AIDS," *Washington Post*, Dec. 1, 2010, http://www.washingtonpost.com/wp-dyn/content/article/2010/11/30/AR2010113005167.html.
2. Walter Rauschenbusch, *Christianity and the Social Crisis* (New York: The Macmillan Company, 1913), 285.
3. Jeffrey Sachs, *The End of Poverty* (New York: Penguin, 2006), 59.
4. Ibid., 60.
5. Ibid., 296, table 1.
6. Dambisa Moyo, *Dead AID* (Vancouver, BC: Douglas & Mcintyre, 2009), 46.
7. Both are correct on certain points, and the issue doesn't have a simple answer.

CHAPTER 23
1. TOMS, "One for One Giving Report," August 24, 2011, http://www.toms.com/media/files/8.24.11_GivingReport_Update.pdf.
2. IEG Sponsorship Report, "Sponsorship Spending on Causes to Total $1.55 Billion This Year," 2009, http://www.sponsorship.com.

3. "Civic-Minded Millennials Prepared to Reward or Punish Companies Based on Commitment to Social Causes," *The 2006 Cone Millennial Cause Study,* (Boston: Cone Communications, Inc., October 2006), http://www.csrwire.com/press_ releases/19346-Civic-Minded-Millennials-Prepared-to-Reward-or-Punish-Companies-Based-on-Commitment-to-Social-Causes.

4. Stephen Mansfield, *The Search for God and Guinness* (Nashville: Thomas Nelson, 2009).

5. Matthew Bishop and Michael Green, *Philanthrocapitalism* (London: Bloomsbury USA, 2008), 6.

6. Mennonite Central Committee played a key role in launching Ten Thousand Villages and the Church of the Brethren, which launched SERRV, credited with being among the first organizations to promote fair trade. They are founders of the World Fair Trade Organization and helped establish standards for fair-trade labeling.

7. Adam Smith, *The Wealth of Nations* (Hollywood, FL: Simon & Brown, 2010).

8. The total value of US imports from China in 2009.

9. "I am Woman, Hear Me Shop." *Bloomberg Businessweek*, February 2005, http://www.businessweek.com/bwdaily/dnflash/feb2005/ nf20050214_9413_db_082.htm.

10. This is the most conservative estimate of Christian wealth.

CHAPTER 24

1. Edward C. Green, "Faith-Based Organizations: Contributions to HIV Prevention," Harvard Center for Population and Development Studies, USAID, September 2003, 4.

2. Augustus Neander, *Tertullian*, "The History of the Christian Religion and Church During First Three Centuries," (Google Books, 1843).

3. Bob Tortora, "Africans' Confidence in Institutions—Which Country Stands Out?", *Gallup News Service*, January 18, 2007, http://www.gallup.com/poll/26176/africans-confidence-institutions-which-country-stands-out.aspx.

4. Dualism is a view that sees human identity in two parts—the physical body (which is the only thing we can see, observe,

measure) and a mysterious Casper the ghost that rides along with the body (but probably doesn't exist anyway). This is in contrast to the Christian understanding of holism which sees human identity as an integrated whole—an inseparable being of physical, spiritual, and relational dimensions. For a dualist, "separate time, separate place" is perfectly logical and possible. Those who see people as whole and integrated creatures believe all aspects of human need are interrelated.

5. This "telling" assumes a culturally sensitive and appropriate way of inviting and, as said, never a manipulation or coercion.

CHAPTER 25

1. Scot McKnight, *Fasting* (Nashville: Thomas Nelson, 2010), 105.
2. Ibid.

CHAPTER 26

1. "Keeping up with the Gateses," *The Economist*, June 17, 2010, http://www.economist.com/node/16381387.
2. Luisa Kroll, "Forbes' richest in US are still feeling recession," *Forbes*, September 21, 2010, http://www.nbcnews.com/id/39308639/#.Um22-pRARqK.
3. For specific examples, visit www.givingpledge.org.
4. Matthew Bishop and Michael Green, *Philanthrocapitalism* (London: Bloomsbury USA, 2008), 51.
5. "Frequently Asked Questions," *The Giving Pledge*, July 1, 2013, http://givingpledge.org/pdf/GivingPledge_FAQ.pdf .
6. Christian Smith, Michael O. Emerson, and Patricia Snell, *Passing the Plate* (New York: Oxford University Press, 2008), 11.
7. It may be highly taboo to "question the authenticity of their claim to be Christian"; however, if one does not give anything to any person, cause, or church, and does not even participate in a local fellowship, then how can that person be a follower/disciple/imitator of Jesus Christ, whose generosity and commitment to community and fellowship deeply characterized His life? I think Matthew 25 makes this discernment clear.
8. This term basically means giving 10 percent after tax for most of

us. It assumes an average salary of $41,967 adjusted down for an after-tax income of $29,377 to yield annual giving at $2,937. It then allows for 10 percent of Christians to be unable to give due to economic hardship, but it also allows for existing levels of "freewill" giving (giving above 10 percent) to remain.

9. Christian Smith, Michael O. Emerson, and Patricia Snell, *Passing the Plate* (New York: Oxford University Press, 2008), 27

10. Jeffrey Sachs, *The End of Poverty* (New York: Penguin, 2006), 59.

11. Christian Smith, Michael O. Emerson, and Patricia Snell, *Passing the Plate* (New York: Oxford University Press, 2008), 55.

12. Ibid.

13. Philip Jenkins, *The Next Christendom: The Coming of Global Christianity* (New York: Oxford University Press, 2002).

14. David Platt, *Radical* (Colorado Springs: Multnomah Books, 2010).

15. John Calvin, *Commentary on the Epistles of Paul the Apostle to the Corinthians*, trans. John Pringle (Grand Rapids: Baker Book, 2003), 1:297.

16. John Calvin, *Calvin: Institutes of the Christian Religion*, ed. John T. McNeill, trans. Ford Lewis Battles (Philadelphia: Westminster Press, 1960), 2:1098.

17. You may already give 10 percent or more, and I am reminded of advice from a book called *Nudge* that says, "If you want to nudge people into socially desirable behavior, do not, by any means, let them know that their current actions are better than the social norm." (Richard H. Thaler and Cass Sunstein, *Nudge: Improving Decisions about Health, Wealth, and Happiness,* (New York: Penguin, 2009), 74.) I hope that advice doesn't apply in this case as you have experienced the joy of generosity and will let your light shine so that others may glorify God and be inspired to join your example for the good of the kingdom.

18. Matthew Bishop and Michael Green, *Philanthrocapitalism* (London: Bloomsbury USA, 2008), 12.

CHAPTER 27

1. Zach Hunter, *Be the Change* (Grand Rapids: Zondervan, 2011).

2. Alex Harris and Brett Harris, *Do Hard Things* (Colorado Springs: Multnomah Books, 2008).

3. "Changing the Channel," *The Economist*, Special report section, May 1, 2010, 4. http://www.economist.com/node/15980859.

ABOUT COMPASSION INTERNATIONAL

On a war-torn Korean street in 1952, God moved evangelist Everett Swanson. He moved him with compassion for the "least of these"—the poor and vulnerable orphans of war who had no voice. No advocate. And no hope.

Over six decades later, Compassion International serves over 1.5 million children in some of the world's most impoverished communities. Compassion tackles the root causes of poverty in the lives of these children through long-term, Christ-centered child development. Each of these children experience a Compassion Child Development Center where they come to be known, loved and protected.

Compassion's Mission Statement

In response to the Great Commission, Compassion exists as an advocate for children, to release them from their spiritual, economic, social and physical poverty, and enable them to become responsible and fulfilled Christian adults.

The Compassion Distinctives

Christ-Centered. Jesus Christ is at the heart of
   Compassion's ministry. Each child in Compassion's
   program has the opportunity to hear the gospel in an age-
   appropriate and culturally relevant way.
Child-Focused. Compassion is dedicated to meeting the
   unique physical, economic, social and spiritual needs
   of children trapped in poverty. Surrounding children
   with caring adults, the love of a sponsor, and a strategic
   development curriculum provides them with the role
   modeling and nurture that leads to transformation.
Church-Based. The church is God's chosen instrument
   to bring hope to a hurting world and deliver justice to
   the poor and oppressed. Each church with a Compassion
   child development center is carefully selected, equipped
   and unleashed for excellent ministry. It is the grassroots
   reach and firsthand knowledge of the families in their
   neighborhood that enable these churches to minister
   personally and effectively to children.

Compassion Content

God nurtures a special relationship with the poor and oppressed.

Nowhere do the forces of injustice and poverty conspire to do more damage than in the vulnerable lives of children. That's why Compassion develops highly specific content to enable Christians understand the damage poverty inflicts. The potential of children who can be released for its grip. And to exalt the overwhelming power of the church to transform the lives of children.

To sponsor a child, visit Compassion.com
Contact us at 1.800.336.7676

APPRECIATION

Special thanks to the team in the president's office at Compassion International—to Carrie Smith, Ashley Higgins, Gayle Call, Mary Lou Elliott, Dinah Meyer, Angie Lathrop, and Angelina Dieleman for their prayers, encouragement, and support. I also wish to thank the members of the Publishing at Compassion team, Creative Blue, Different Drummer, and Somersault—in particular, Tim Frye, Erik Lokkesmoe, Kurt Birky, John Topliff, and Dave Lambert. I am deeply indebted to my friends and mentors and express my gratitude for their outstanding personal as well as professional counsel, reviews, insights, and encouragement—Paul Moede, Mark Yeadon, David Dahlin, Tony Neeves, and Wess Stafford. And thanks to my friends and family for kindness and feedback—to Robin and Brett Hersma, George and Catherine Bocox, Jason and Diana Douglas (and all the staff at the Hideaway for taking care of me during the intense season of writing).

I gigantically express my gratitude to my adverb-hating editor, Caleb Seeling, at Samizdat Creative Services. Thank you for your good humor, your heart for the cause, and for your ruthless wielding of the anti-redundancy axe. But please return my poetic license because rocks can be angry, and people can slump along!!! (You are not allowed to edit those !!! either!!!)

I thank each of my sons, Micah, Jacob, Samuel, and Levi for being awesome guys, a lot of fun, and for joining me in the mission.

Above all I couldn't have written this or done much of anything useful in life without the love and constant devotion of my dear wife, Bethany. Ever since the day I met you, I have not stopped thanking Him for bringing you into my life. God used you to rescue me and still rescues me through your joy. Keep smiling.